Answers to my Evolutionist Friends

HOW LIFE BEGAN

THOMAS F. HEINZE

CHICK
PUBLICATIONS

For a complete list of distributors nearest you call us at (909) 987-0771 or visit us on the world wide web at **www.chick.com**

Copyright © 2002 by Thomas F. Heinze

Published by:
CHICK PUBLICATIONS
P. O. Box 3500, Ontario, CA 91761-1019 USA
Tel: (909) 987-0771 • Fax: (909) 941-8128
www.chick.com
E Mail: postmaster@chick.com

Printed in the United States of America

ISBN: 0-758904-79-7

Contents

Contents (continued)

CHAPTER 4
Pulling It All Together 109

CHAPTER 5
The Message 137

Introduction

Is there a God who created life? Most people used to think so, largely because the Bible says so, from the well known first chapter of Genesis, to this reference in the last book that says God "...created heaven, and the things that therein are, and the earth, and the things that therein are, and the sea, and the things which are therein..." (Revelation 10:6). Now many are not so sure life was created. The schools and media have long taught that life could have simply come about by ever more complex chemicals building up. No Creator necessary! But how good is their evidence to back up this idea?

Hang on tight for the ride of your life. You will be amazed. I have been following this subject for most of my adult life and I want to share it with you. We are going to follow the evidence into key areas of the first life controversy, where you will see it stripped nude of the seductive interpretations that can paint black as if it were white. Important statements will be backed by quotes from authorities, usually atheists or evolutionists. When I point out an important statement that one of them has made, I am calling your attention to that statement, not implying that its author and I agree on everything.

First a necessary explanation:

• Creationists generally believe the Bible's explanation that God created a number of basic groups of animals and plants as described in the first part of Genesis. They believe that while God created each group with the possibility of a good deal of variation, they brought forth according to their own kind. (Cats bring forth cats, not dogs).

• Evolution can mean many things. Some use the word to refer to any change at all. Obviously the creation/evolution debate is not about that kind of a definition. Creationists agree that many changes take place, but disagree with the theory of evolution when it is used to mean that a gradual progression from molecules to man produced all living things by natural means, that is, without the involvement of an intelligent Creator.

• The question of **how life began** is different than that of why one kind of animal differs from another. However, many books that expound the theory of evolution also promote naturalistic theories of how life began. They make a rather smooth transition from atoms to Adam; from molecules to man. They suggest a hypothetical first cell which is a step before what we usually think of as evolution. If proved, it would be the step on which all the rest of life depends. It is also a step which can more easily be put to the test because it depends on scientific principles rather than on whether or not some animal happened to leave fossils. For these reasons, I thought it would be good to begin my series, *Answers to My Evolutionist Friends* with this book, *How Life Began*. Later, I hope to provide *Answers to My Evolutionist Friends* in other areas of the creation/evolution controversy.

Now, put on your detective hat, grab your magnifying glass, and let's follow the evidence about how life began, and see where it leads.

1

Proteins and Time

Design or Chance

I lived in Italy for 34 years, and could often spot Roman ruins, even at a distance while driving down the freeway at Italian speeds. The most massive Roman amphitheaters were basically one brick on top of another. Roman bricks are flat, about an inch thick and a foot long. Their design is very simple, and objects with simple designs are more apt to happen by chance than those that are more complex. However, in spite of the simplicity of the bricks, they, and the huge complex structures the Romans built from them, are obviously products of intelligent design.

What clues can help determine whether cells and the things they are made of were designed by an intelligent Creator or fell together without any intelligent input?

Is the Cell Simple?

Once, when my boys were little, they called me over to look in their toy microscope. As I shared their excitement at the sight of some single celled creatures, little blobs moving around in a drop of water, my thoughts turned to the microscopes of Darwin's time. I realized that scientists in those days must have thought that blobs like these really were simple.

Evolutionists notice that all cells have more or less the same basic parts and conclude that they all evolved from one first cell. There is another possibility, the one that comes to mind when we notice that thousands of different Roman structures, from amphitheaters to aqueducts, are made of bricks stacked one on top of another. They did not evolve one from another, they were all products of intelligent design.

Even the simplest cell is millions of times more complex than the Roman Coliseum. Its complexity makes it difficult to believe that there was no intelligence involved in its production.

When proposing the spontaneous appearance of the first cell, many "science" books still talk about the apparently simple blobs that people could see in the primitive microscopes of long ago. Is it possible that they want to avoid facing the problem of how the fantastic complexity of even the simplest cell could have come about?

The Origin of Life

For years, those who believed that the first life formed with no God involved taught that simple chemicals became concentrated in the ocean, making an organic broth of ever more complex chemicals out of which life emerged.

Some call this idea "chemical evolution." This is a straightforward term which brings to mind simple chemicals developing into more complex chemicals, and ties the formation of the first life to the rest of the theory of evolution. "Abiogenesis," however, is now the preferred word for this theory. It is a bit confusing because the word is made up of three Greek roots: "not," "life," and "generate," which would seem to mean, "There is no spontaneous generation of life." It is used today to mean just the opposite: "The production of living organisms from non-living matter."[1]

The theory that life began when proteins, DNA, and RNA were formed by chance, or by some sort of chemical evolution and somehow got together, has been taught to enough generations that not only atheists accept it, but many who believe in God feel this must be the way He created life.

Let's dive in and examine the steps in the formation of the first life as taught to the last few generations. Then we will examine the more recent variations of the theme.

Amino Acids, the Building Blocks of Proteins

Proteins, the main ingredients of living things, are made of amino acids. Stanley Miller's experiment in 1953 became famous because it showed a way in which amino acids could be formed apart from already living cells. (See Figure A.) It was hailed as a way that life could have begun without a Creator, and is still honored by most biology texts. If amino acids could be formed apart from cells, why not protein, DNA, and everything else a cell needs?

---

[1]Random House Webster's College Dictionary, 2000, p. 3.

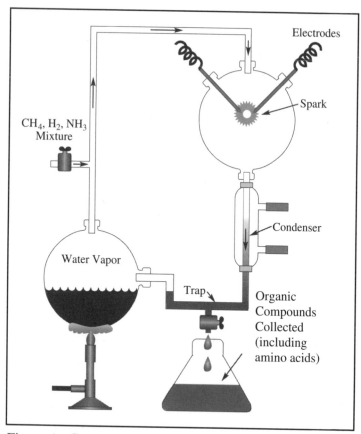

Figure A **Stanley Miller's apparatus for making amino acids.**

Miller's first step was to create an atmosphere containing the chemicals of which amino acids are composed. He then passed a spark through his chosen atmosphere. Small amounts of amino acids were produced.[1]

Does this mean life could form?

There were problems:

• Only around half of the twenty amino acids from which proteins are formed were produced.

• A much larger quantity of other chemicals, mostly useless tars, was also formed.

• Had there been oxygen in the atmosphere it would have combined with the other chemicals in the atmosphere so that no amino acids would have formed. Some researchers think oxygen was there all along:

> "But many researchers now hold that the ancient Earth's atmosphere, compared with the earlier view, had more oxygen and less hydrogen—as the atmosphere does today. Amino acids don't form as readily under that condition as they did in the 1953 experiment, and when they do form, they tend to break apart."[2]

• After the first spark had produced amino acids, additional sparks would have broken them down again. To prevent this, Miller built a trap into the apparatus to take

---

[1]Stanley L. Miller, *From Primordial Soup to the Prebiotic Beach,* www.gene.com/ae/WN/NM/miller.html, 1996.

[2]Gorman, Jessica, "Cosmic Chemistry Gets Creative." *Science News,* 05/19/2001, Vol. 159, Issue 20, p. 318. See also: "New Evidence on Evolution of Early Atmosphere and Life," *Bulletin of the American Meteorological Society,* Vol. 63, Nov. 1982, p. 1329; Clemmey and Badham, "Oxygen in the Precambrian Atmosphere: An Evaluation of the Geological Evidence," *Geology,* Vol. 10, March 1982, pp. 141, 145.

newly formed amino acids out of the cycle and save them from destruction. The trap is usually more or less ignored, but its presence means Miller's experiment does not show what might happen in nature. The trap ensured the survival of amino acids. In nature, where there is no trap, if any amino acids were created, the quantity which survived would have been negligible. That is why Miller included the trap.

After the first spark had produced amino acids, additional sparks would have broken them down again. To prevent this, Miller built a trap into the apparatus to take newly formed amino acids out of the cycle and save them from destruction. The trap is usually more or less ignored, but its presence means that Miller's experiment does not show what might happen in nature.

Many books suggest the contrary, that in nature, lightning passing through the right atmosphere would have formed enough of the necessary amino acids to combine to make all the essential proteins of the first living cell. At the same time, DNA and/or RNA were imagined to have formed and to have gotten together with the proteins. The first living cell is claimed to have been the result, but was that possible?

One huge problem is that amino acids produced like this will not work in living things. Amino acids come in two forms called right and left-handed because one is a mirror image of the other. Proteins which contain all left-handed amino acids will connect correctly with the surrounding proteins. However, if a right-handed amino acid is included, the shape of the protein is changed and the protein will not work in a living cell. If proteins were first formed of the R and L mixture of amino acids produced in Miller's experiment, it would have been impossible for them to connect to one another.

To understand this, think of a jigsaw puzzle already put together and lying on a table. Take one piece out of the middle, turn it upside down and try to fit it back where you took it out. It won't fit because what should be at the right end of the piece is now at the left and vice versa. Even one right-handed amino acid changes the shape of the protein in which it is found. In the place where that acid is found, the protein sticks out where it should dip in and in where it should stick out.

Whenever amino acids are formed outside of living cells, they are always half left-handed (L amino acids) and half right-handed (D amino acids). The mixture is called a racemic mixture. Both L and D amino acids take part equally well in ordinary chemical reactions, but in *living* organisms the shape is so important that only proteins made entirely of L amino acids will connect properly, and they never happen in nature outside of living cells.

People who believe life started without a Creator seldom mention this problem, but here it is from a scientist who claims to have found crystals which will separate small amounts of amino acids to an "exciting" 55 to 45 percent mixture:

> "The puzzle is that amino acids, the constituents of proteins, occur in two chemically identical forms that have structures mirroring each other like two gloves. Most chemical processes yield left-and right-handed

> amino acids in equal amounts yet life forms contain
> left-handed amino acids almost exclusively."[1]

Since it would take 100% left-handed amino acids to make a useful protein, Gorman's percentages (55% to 45%), though slightly better than the usual fifty fifty, would not help make proteins. The importance he attributes to even a small increase in the percentage of left-handed amino acids helps you understand that living things need left-handed amino acids.

It gets worse. Pure left-handed amino acids spontaneously become "racemic." That is, after they have been made in cells or in labs, they start switching back to their natural state, which is half left and half right-handed. One at a time, they switch from their current handedness and become a mixture of both left and right-handed amino acids.

Over the years, schoolbooks have made it sound like amino acids such as those produced by Miller's experiment would have come together to make proteins. By doing this, they have helped convince millions of students that life formed with no Creator. But should our schools be leading students to believe things that are untrue to favor one religious belief over another? Certainly the faith that proteins suitable for life could be formed by a mixture of right and left-handed amino acids is not sustained by the observations or experiments of science.

To sum things up, schoolbooks that report on Miller's experiment usually withhold the following vital evidence:

---

[1] J. Gorman, "Rocks May Have Given a Hand to Life," *Science News,* May 5, 2001, p. 276.

• Miller's experiment produced only about half of the amino acids used by the proteins of living things.

• Amino acids produced like this are mixed right and left-handed. They cannot be used to form proteins that will work in cells.

Making Proteins

The fact that Miller became famous when he was able to make half of the necessary amino acids under conditions which might have occurred in nature, attracted other scientists to try the next step: putting amino acids together to make proteins, the main ingredients of living cells.

...not one of the complex proteins of living things is ever formed under conditions similar to those in nature except by already living cells.

Since no way has been found by which nature could ever provide all left-handed amino acids, scientists purchased all twenty types of fresh left-handed amino acids from chemical supply houses. They then made the perfect organic broth themselves. However, the amino acids would not link together to form proteins. In spite of the tremendous rewards that await the winner, not one of the complex proteins of living things is ever formed under conditions similar to those in nature except by already living cells.

Today, most school biology books still use Miller's experiment to help convince kids that life could have formed by natural causes. But I found a biology textbook which admits that amino acids in an organic broth could not get together to form proteins:

> "Scientists have not been able to cause amino acids dissolved in water to join together to form proteins. The energy-requiring chemical reactions that join amino acids are reversible and do not occur spontaneously in water. However, most scientists no longer argue that the first proteins assembled spontaneously. Instead, they now propose that the initial macromolecules were composed of RNA, and that RNA later catalyzed the formation of proteins."[1]

I would like to say that it was for the sake of honesty and truth that these authors have finally revealed the fact that amino acids won't form proteins in water, but they clearly state the reason: "most scientists no longer argue that the first proteins assembled spontaneously. Instead, they now propose that the initial macromolecules were composed of RNA, and that RNA later catalyzed the formation of proteins." Most of the books I have examined are not yet openly admitting that proteins "do not occur spontaneously in water." In fact, many lead the reader to believe the opposite.

For years creationists were almost alone in objecting to this untruth being taught as science. They were joined, however, as far back as 1981 by a well known scientist who believes in evolution and is one of the top men in first life research. He wrote:

> "Since science has not the vaguest idea how (proteins)

---

[1]George B. Johnson, Peter H. Raven, *Biology, Principles & Explorations,* Holt, Rinhehart and Winston, 1996, p. 235.

originated, it would only be honest to admit this to students, the agencies funding research, and the public."[1]

Proteins, like houses, do not build themselves. A cell, however, would be better compared to a city than a house because, just as it takes many houses to make a city, the simplest of cells are composed of at least hundreds of proteins. Proteins, like houses, soon break down, so even if some proteins could build themselves (which they cannot) a concentration of all the needed proteins could never build up.

In addition, their left-handed amino acids switch toward half left and half right-handed even after they have been made into proteins. To function in a living cell, each protein must have its own peculiar three-dimensional shape. Usually if even one right-handed amino acid is included, it changes the shape of the protein enough that it cannot function properly. In a living cell a protein in which an amino acid has switched handedness is chopped up and replaced with a new one. If the impossible had happened, and a first protein had built up, some of its amino acids would have switched to right-handed while it was waiting for the other proteins to form. As soon as the first amino acid had switched, the protein in which it was found would have become useless.

The spontaneous formation of proteins, which for years was taught in school textbooks, among other places, was unscientific. It proposed not just one, but a long series of chance happenings that could never happen:

---

[1]Hubert P. Yockey, "Self Organization Origin of Life Scenarios and Information Theory," *Journal of Theoretical Biology,* 91:13-31, 1981.

• The amino acids formed by passing a spark through the correct atmosphere would be suitable for making proteins (all the essential types, and all left-handed).

• These amino acids would come together to form an organic broth from which proteins would form.

• The first proteins, once formed, could wait millions of years for the formation of the remaining proteins necessary to form a cell.

• The ocean would allow the right proteins to concentrate in one place and not wash them apart. (Or, as some claim, the entire sea would have been filled with organic broth).[1]

• DNA and/or RNA would also form in nature and get together with all the necessary proteins. A cell wall would form around them.

A schoolbook stated one reason why proteins are not formed in nature outside of cells: "The energy-requiring chemical reactions that join amino acids are reversible and do not occur spontaneously in water." Another reason is that to form proteins, the amino acids must be linked together in a particular order. Let's use a gold chain as an analogy. Gold, like amino acids, can be found in nature, yet even though the links of most gold chains can be inserted in any order, chains made of many links of gold are never produced by the random forces of nature. Proteins are much more difficult because their amino acids must be linked together in a particular order, and that order is different for each protein. DNA not only tells the cell how to link amino acids together, but also specifies the order in which each amino acid must be linked.

---

[1] K. Arms and P. Camp, *Biology*, Holt Rinehart and Winston, 1979, p. 158.

Some claim that proteins can form because amino acids have a natural tendency to link up in a particular order. This idea is in error because in that case only that one protein could be produced. It is only by following the instructions in DNA that the amino acids can link in the right orders to form each of the different proteins.

Why did anyone believe that cells could evolve from proteins when not even one of the proteins of living things can be made by chance? Parents and children trusted schoolbooks which manipulated the evidence to support a a philosophic/religious viewpoint which was based on a faith commitment, not on scientific evidence. When it became obvious that no scientific solution to the problem of protein formation would be found, a psychological solution was seized upon.

Billions of Years

In the past, many people were convinced that the first life could have been formed by chance because the time available was so incomprehensibly vast. The famous Harvard biology professor George Wald popularized this idea in 1955 with his famous quote:

> "Time is the hero of the plot. The time with which we have to deal is of the order of two billion years... Given so much time the 'impossible' becomes possible, the possible probable, and the probable virtually certain. One has only to wait: time itself performs miracles."[1]

1George Wald, "The Origin of Life," in *The Physics and Chemistry of Life,* 1955, p. 12.

To understand probabilities, we often use the illustration of flipping a coin. If you want a penny to come up heads a thousand times in a row, there will be more chance of it happening if you flip it for two billion years than if you flip it for an hour. Wald has something like this in mind.

Time, however, does not increase the chance that the penny would turn into a nickel, a dime, a quarter and a silver dollar which would then sprout wings and fly off together into the sunset doing aerobatic stunts in a tight formation. Time does increase the probability of something happening if it can happen, but the statement "time itself performs miracles" is false. Wald understood that if one took the evidence at face value, it would be impossible not only for chance to put together a first cell, but even for it to put together any one of the many necessary proteins. To keep from resorting to God, he needed to find something else which could do miracles. His quote, "time itself performs miracles" seemed to explain how things that could not happen without miracles could have happened. His whole statement seemed possible because part of the statement was true.

If someone says that a frog turned into a prince, we immediately recognize it as a fairy tale. But when respected teachers and textbooks tell us that in many millions of years frogs did in fact turn into princes, the idea somehow sounds scientific. Billions of years are even better. This book, however, is not concerned with how convincing billions of years can be made to sound, but with, "Could they perform the miracle of life?" Evaluate the evidence for yourself.

If amino acids and other chemicals produced in nature did not break down but accumulated to form an organic broth, in time the chemicals that are produced more easily and those that break down more slowly would have predominated. Consequently, some of life's most necessary chemicals would have been rare or non-existent.

Outside of living cells, all left-handed amino acids do not form under natural conditions; much less get together to form proteins. They do, however, switch spontaneously to a useless mixture of left and right-handed.[1] This fact is sometimes used to help police identify a body if they need to know its age at the time of death.[2] Unlike the proteins in the rest of our bodies, those in our teeth are not eliminated when one of their amino acids turns right-handed. Because of this, right-handed amino acids build up in teeth, and the percentage that have changed to right-handed can be measured. Professor Ohtani, one of the world's foremost experts in forensic medicine, referring to aspartic acid, the amino acid which changes from left to right-handed most rapidly, writes that at 37 degrees Celsius (body temperature), "it will take about 17 years to change 1% of L-aspartic acid into D-form." (D stands for right-handed).

He believes the ocean temperature at the time life formed might have been quite cold, around 15° C. He says

---

[1]John Mackay and Diane Eager, *Search for the Origin of Life,* published by Creation Research, Australia, 3rd edition, 1998, p. 4.
[2]Ohtani S. "Estimation of Age from the Teeth..." *American Journal of Forensic Med. Pathol,* 1995, 16:3, pp. 238-242; Ohtani S, and Katsuichi Y., "Age Estimation Using the Racemization of Amino Acid in Human Dentine," *Journal of Forensic Sciences,* May, 1991, p. 792-800; same, July 1992, p. 1061-1067.

that at this temperature "…it is calculated that it takes 75,188 years to change 1% of the L-form aspartic acid into D-aspartic acid…"[1]

Not 1%, but just one right-handed amino acid in a protein usually blocks that protein's biological activity, so if by some miracle the ocean started out full of all left-handed amino acids, in a relatively short time far too many amino acids would have become right-handed to permit the formation of proteins.

A Mammoth Disappointment

I still remember the dramatic announcement that an entire mammoth, reported to have lived between ten and twenty thousand years ago, had been found frozen in Siberia. Its huge tusks, shown sticking out of a great block of ice, were flown by helicopter to a place where scientists could work on the beast. Freezing is the method used in laboratories to preserve cells for artificial insemination, and it was hoped that, frozen as it was, at least some of its trillions of strands of DNA would have been preserved intact. Then perhaps the animal could be cloned, or a sex cell would be found which could be bred with a modern elephant.

After the very hopeful first announcement, not much was said in America, so I quote from *The Moscow Times:*

"Those reports have subsequently been proven false. The block actually contains only scattered remains, including bones, fur and tissue. Scientists say the find holds nothing especially valuable, and certainly

---

[1]From a private letter from Professor Ohtani, 12/15/2000.

nothing that could be cloned. 'Elementary knowledge of physics rules that out.' For cloning to work, Tikhonov said, it is necessary to find an intact cell containing a whole segment of DNA. Since water makes up around 80 percent of cells, frozen cells necessarily expand and rupture. 'It's impossible to find an intact cell in a block that has been frozen more than 1,000 years.'"[1]

The mammoth was a big disappointment for those who believed that frozen DNA would last for very long periods of time.

Scientists can, however, study DNA even when it is quite old using a method called gene amplification. They only need to find pieces long enough to contain around 140 base pairs (rungs of the DNA ladder).[2] (By way of comparison, a human cell contains around three billion base pairs of DNA). A strand of DNA is incredibly thin, so after a cell dies, its DNA soon breaks into shorter pieces. RNA breaks down even more rapidly.

Scientists needed a way to determine whether DNA found in old specimens like the mammoth, dinosaurs, etc. had come from the specimens themselves, the hands of the people who had handled them, or bacteria from ground water which had passed through, etc. It was discovered that the amino acids in proteins break down from all left-handed to right and left-handed at about the same rate that the DNA

---

[1]Gregory Feifer, "A Mammoth Pursuit," *The Moscow Times,* 01/05/2001.
[2]Hendrik N. Poinar, Matthais Hoss, Jeffrey L. Badda, Svante Paabo, "Amino Acid Racemization and the Preservation of Ancient DNA," *Science,* Vol. 272, 10 May, 1996, p. 864.

strand breaks into pieces. Therefore, if some of the amino acids in the proteins of an old specimen have already become right-handed, and complete strands of DNA are found, they they are not from the specimen, but are recent arrivals.[1]

Amino acids and DNA are always breaking down, but it happens more rapidly in the presence of both water and heat.[2] Seeds that need to keep their DNA intact until the next spring or longer, often have a natural waterproof coating.

The "organic broth" from which the first cell is claimed to have come is mostly water. This would speed up the breakdown of DNA, RNA, amino acids, and proteins. It would be one of the worst places to try to build up a concentration of these substances. If, over billions of years, a protein molecule could have formed, it would have broken down long before the hundreds of other proteins needed to form a cell could have formed.

Stanley Miller, writing about the hot water vents in the ocean floor where many claim the first life formed, states:

> "Submarine vents don't make organic compounds, they decompose them. ...the entire ocean goes through those vents in 10 million years. So all of the organic compounds get zapped every ten million years. If all the polymers and other goodies that you make get destroyed, it means life has to start early and rapidly. If you look at the process in detail, it

---

[1] Poinar, "Amino Acid Racemization...", *Science,* Vol. 272, 5/9/96 p. 864.
[2] Poinar, "Amino Acid Racemization...", *Science,* Vol. 272, 5/9/96 p. 864.

seems that long periods of time are detrimental,
rather than helpful."[1]

Wald thought that two billion years had been available to
make "the impossible possible." However, as more fossils
have been found, animals that once fit neatly in a particular
evolutionary segment of time are often found also in older
or younger strata and less and less time (if any) remains for
evolution.

A modern Nobel prize winning evolutionist explains that
fossils of advanced forms of life have been found in strata
dated three billion years older than Wald thought possible.

"Advanced forms of life existed on earth at least 3.55
billion years ago.... On the other hand, it is believed
that our young planet, still in the throes of volcanic
eruptions and battered by falling comets and
asteroids, remained inhospitable to life for about half
a billion years after its birth... some 4.55 billion
years ago. This leaves a window of perhaps 200-300
million years for the appearance of life on earth.... It
is now generally agreed that if life arose spontaneously
by natural processes... it must have arisen fairly
quickly, more in a matter of millennia or centuries,
perhaps even less, than in millions of years."[2]

His point is important. Evolutionists believe that a half
billion years were needed for the earth to accumulate
enough meteorites, etc. to arrive at about its present size

---

[1]Stanley L. Miller, *From Primordial Soup to the Prebiotic Beach,*
www.gene.com/ae/WN/NM/miller.html, 1996.
[2]Christian de Duve, "The Beginning of Life on Earth," *American
Scientist,* Vol. 83, Sept-Oct. 1995, p. 428.

and then cool sufficiently for life to form. Evolutionists in Wald's time believed that after two billion years of abiogenesis or chemical evolution, the first life formed in or slightly before the Cambrian period which they date at a half billion years ago. Radioactive dating now puts "advanced life forms" already on earth 3.5 billion years ago; three billion years before Wald had thought. What were these "advanced life forms like?" "…surprisingly similar to modern organisms…"[1] Many scientists believe that for the animals that left these fossils to have developed to their "advanced" stage they must have already evolved for millions or billions of years. Because they demonstrated this "advanced" stage of evolution, de Duve says the window of opportunity for chemicals to get together and form life was very short, "more in a matter of millennia or centuries, perhaps even less, than in millions of years."

The Rare Earth, a more recent book which also supports rapid formation of a first cell, estimates the cooling time a bit longer and cuts around 200 million years off the time de Duve thought might be available:

> "By about 3.8 billion years ago that heavy cosmic bombardment ended, and by 3.5 billion years ago we find the first fossilized evidence of life."[2]

On page 57 these authors say:

> "The oldest fossils that we do find are from rocks

---

[1] Miller/Levine, *Biology, the Living Science,* Prentice Hall Biology textbook, 1998, p. 398.

[2] Peter D. Ward, Donald Brownlee, *Rare Earth, Why Complex Life is Uncommon in the Universe,* 2000, p. 95.

about 3.6 billion years of age, and they look identical
to bacteria still on Earth today."

The oldest fossils that have been found looked like fully
evolved modern bacteria, not like they would still need
billions of years to get to that stage.

On page 87 these authors say "These first fossils are
filamentous..." which means organized into a ribbon like
shape.

Since evolutionists think that much time would have
been required after life started to evolve to this stage, even
schoolbooks now state that the first life would have to have
arisen rapidly:

"Soon after the earth's surface cooled, life arose in
the ancient seas. The first organisms to appear on the
planet were bacteria...."[1]

Pushing the formation of life back when the water had
not had much time to cool reminds us that the warmer the
water, the more rapidly the chemicals from which cells are
made would have broken down.

A college level biology text published in 1979 shows
what evolutionists thought at that time:

"The other important requirement for the origin of
life is plenty of time. The events necessary for the
beginnings of life were extremely unlikely."[2]

Unlikely events might be more likely to happen in lots
of time but modern books say this "important requirement"
could not have been met. Does that mean abiogenesis was

---

[1]Holt, Annotated Teacher's Edition, *Biology, Visualizing Life,* 1994, p. 203.
[2]K. Arms and P. Camp, *Biology,* Holt Rinehart and Winston, 1979, p. 156.

testable and has been shown to be false? No. Those who believe in abiogenesis have simply dropped "plenty of time" as an "important requirement for the origin of life." Now they just say that it happened rapidly.

It would be difficult to test in a laboratory a "miracle" which happened because it had two billion years. Things that happen rapidly, however, should be easier to check out. Scientists, in fact, have dedicated themselves to doing tests, hoping to show that the first life could have come about with no intelligent design. So far they have only shown that it could not have happened in the ways they thought were most likely and checked out first. Since they are gradually eliminating the best possibilities, could we again say that the idea is testable and is being shown to be false? Some say, "No! We will always be able to think of some other way it might have happened." They are making their hypothesis untestable and taking it out of the realm of science.

You may have believed that life began spontaneously from organic broth in two billion years. But such an idea has been abandoned as a mistake. Are you able to work up the same faith that the "impossible became possible," and then evolved to look identical to bacteria still on earth today in only "millennia or centuries, perhaps even less," the time de Duve suggests, or "rapidly" as other authors express it?

Why try?

2

Could Cell Parts Get Together?

Hot Ocean Bottom Vents and the Second Law of Thermodynamics

Many today believe that the first life formed in hot submarine vents where water comes out of the earth in the bottom of the ocean, but there are good reasons why this is unlikely:

> "It is also unlikely that the first living systems formed in a high-temperature environment, because this is where the decomposition of organic compounds proceeds most rapidly."[1]

Heat, like water, causes amino acids, proteins, DNA, and RNA to break down more rapidly.[2]

---

[1]Anthony Keefe, *Grolier Multimedia Encyclopedia*, "Life" 1998.
[2]Hendrik N. Poinar... "Amino Acid Racemization and the Preservation of Ancient DNA," *Science*, Vol. 272, May 10, 1996, p. 864.

M. Levy and the famous Stanley Miller write that tests have been made on the nucleotides which form RNA and DNA. Since each type of nucleotide breaks down at a different speed, if the temperature is that of the boiling point of water at sea level, the half-lives of the various nucleotides range from 19 days to 56 years. If the water is even hotter, at 250 C their speed of breakdown ranges from one minute to 35 minutes.[1]

The crushing pressure at the bottom of the sea allows water to actually come out of the earth this hot without boiling. Some odd small creatures have the ability to live in water this hot, but Miller's observations show that outside of living things, the nucleotides of which DNA and RNA are formed break down rapidly in hot water. Miller believes this would keep them from becoming concentrated enough to get together.

The Second Law of Thermodynamics, one of the fundamental laws of science, contributes to Miller's observations. One way of stating it, called entropy, has been called the mother of all Murphy's Laws. Evolutionist Isaac Asimov referred to this when he wrote:

> "Another way of stating the Second Law, then, is: 'The universe is constantly getting more disorderly.'"[2]

He means the universe as a whole. Not that every local spot within it is becoming more disorderly at any one time,

---

[1]Matthew Levy, Stanley L. Miller, "The Stability of the RNA Bases: Implications for the Origin of Life," *Proceedings of the National Academy of Science,* Vol. 95, p. 7935.

[2]"In the Game of Energy and Thermodynamics You Can't Even Break Even," *Smithsonian Institute Journal,* June 1970, p. 10-11.

but things will tend toward disorder if they are left completely alone. "The universe is constantly getting more disorderly."

The Second Law of Thermodynamics is science. To believe that long ago, ever more complex molecules built up until they were living cells which kept building up in complexity, forming fish, monkeys and men, is not science. No one was there to observe chemicals become ever more complex until a living cell was formed, and the process cannot be reproduced in the lab. Abiogenesis and evolution are imaginative speculations about what happened in prehistoric times. For some, they have also become a religion to defend passionately, but they are not science. Their direction from simple chemicals to the most complex and highly organized organ in the world, the human brain, is the opposite of of a tendency toward disorder. Prof. Lambert has explained how the disorder described by entropy works:

> "Whenever an adequate amount of energy flows through a system of objects, it tends to scatter them."[1]

Entropy is explained by complex mathematical calculations most of us don't understand, so people tend to exaggerate. Some would make it seem that entropy would not allow any complex molecules to form. Actually, energy must be added or many complex molecules can't form at

---

[1]Frank L. Lambert, Professor Emeritus, Occidental College, *The Second Law of Thermodynamics,* www.search.britannica.com/frm_redir.jsp?query=entropy&redir=http:// www.secondlaw.c,Time's Arrow.

all. Other people leave the impression that the energy which is always coming to the earth from the sun would have kept the nucleotides which compose DNA and RNA on the primitive earth from breaking down. However, heat still comes to earth from the sun today, and the components of RNA and DNA really do break down more rapidly in hotter water, just as Miller states.

Miller avoided the possible problems with those who argue Second Law theory. He did not say what the Second Law would or would not do. He just measured what actually happens. The more the components of DNA are heated, the faster they break down. The same is true of amino acids, proteins and RNA. Heat tends to scatter the atoms. Adding undirected energy by increasing the heat favors randomness over order.

Having shown that the rate of breakdown really does increase as the heat increases, Miller suggests that if the water were hot, a cell could not form because the nucleotides, etc. would break down too fast to build enough of a concentration to form RNA or DNA. To give more time for the nucleotides to accumulate, Miller suggests that the temperature of the oceans must have been around freezing. At that temperature the breakdown is much slower.

That is much colder than average ocean temperatures today. However, most people who believe in an old Earth, feel that Earth started out so hot that it took around a half billion years just to cool enough so the heat would not kill any life that might have started to form. Could it have cooled to around freezing that soon?

Compounding the problem of cooling the ocean, radioactive elements in the earth give off heat as they break down. Billions of years ago, when many believe the first life originated, not nearly as much radioactive material would already have broken down, so much more heat would have been added by radioactivity than is being added today. If de Duve was right that the window of time available for life to start was more, "a matter of millennia or centuries, perhaps even less, than in millions of years,"[1] the time would seem to be too short for the oceans to have cooled to almost freezing. Yet Miller suggests that unless it were that cold, nucleotides would not build up. (He is assuming there would have been some way for the nucleotides to form, and that when formed they would get together to make DNA or RNA).

Another observation of nature brings out an additional problem with life starting spontaneously. Brig Klyce calls this "logical entropy."[2] While waiting for a better term for the concept, I will use his and mention the evidence for it right here, below the entropy of the Second Law of Thermodynamics. What I am talking about has to do with the fact that certain patterns are observed to form by ordinary natural processes, and others not to form except by intelligent design.

• We see patterns in the sand on the shore because the water sorts the sand by size and the waves move it back and forth.

---

[1]Christian de Duve, "The Beginning of Life on Earth," *American Scientist,* Vol. 83, Sept-Oct. 1995, p. 428.
[2]Brig Klyce, Cosmic Ancestry, www.panspermia.org/seconlaw.htm.

• We have all marveled at the intricate patterns of crystals, so beautiful in snow flakes viewed under a microscope and in slices of thunder eggs.

However, certain areas of science, notably anthropology, are largely based on the observation that certain other patterns don't happen except by deliberate intelligent design. When an anthropologist finds an ancient library, he recognizes it. The books may be written with ink on skins or papyrus, or pressed into clay when it was soft, but there are recognizable differences between patterns produced by intelligent design to contain written messages and those produced by other natural processes. If not, the whole science of anthropology would long ago have crumbled into the dust.

Archeologists also study ancient dwellings. Things can get fuzzy as you pass from libraries to broken down houses. A truck load of bricks dumped from a dump truck never falls into the shape of a house with mortar holding each brick together. The bricks fall from the truck in a heap on the ground. However, in the course of time, the mortar of even a carefully built house may weather out from the bricks, and the bricks may fall into the more probable position of a heap on the ground. If an ancient house is not broken down, but still holds the shape of a house, archeologists recognize it as something that did not happen by chance. Someone built it.

A beautiful vase is easy to recognize as an artifact made by an intelligent being, but the slightly shaped scrappers used by primitive societies are hard to distinguish from natural rocks. The fact that the distinctives are sometimes blurred does not invalidate the science of anthropology. Some patterns are only caused by intelligent design.

The speculation that concentrated chemicals could organize themselves, get inside a cell membrane, and form a living cell is not scientific. It is contrary to the Laws of Probability, Cause and Effect, the principle of Biogenesis (life only comes from life), to the direction described by the entropy of the Second Law of Thermodynamics, and to the observational evidence which Klyce calls "logical entropy."

The belief that the first cell came about when very complex hard to form substances: RNA, proteins, etc. somehow formed, and then became concentrated in a hot organic broth is in conflict with scientific principles:

• The complex molecules which form the components of life tend not to form, but to break down in the presence of water. The hotter the water, the faster they break down, and the less their chance of becoming concentrated enough to get together.

• The speculation that concentrated chemicals could organize themselves, get inside a cell membrane, and form a living cell is not scientific. It is contrary to the Laws of Probability, Cause and Effect, the principle of Biogenesis (life only comes from life), to the direction described by the entropy of the Second Law of Thermodynamics, and to the observational evidence which Klyce calls "logical entropy." It is also contrary to experimental evidence: Neither proteins nor DNA nor RNA form in nature outside of living cells; not even the nucleotides of which DNA and

RNA are made will form under simulated natural conditions. The chemicals DNA and RNA are so complex and hard to form that at this point, complete strands cannot even be made in the lab. Even if a cell could be formed, it would only function if it contained information programmed very specifically to direct that particular type of cell.

Do Proteins in the Ocean Concentrate?

Authors who believe that the first life started in the ocean usually claim that proteins, DNA, RNA, and lipids formed in the ocean, and became concentrated to form an organic broth. In real life, none of these substances form by themselves, particularly in water. According to many books promoting evolution, however, they did, and then got together to form the first living cell. Other authors say they would not concentrate:

> "The idea of such a 'soup' containing all desired organic molecules in concentrated form in the ocean has been a misleading concept against which objections were raised early."[1]

If they did not both form and concentrate, the necessary substances could never have gotten together to make the first cell. (Other environments for the spontaneous formation of life have also been suggested. We will deal with them as well).

Concentration or dispersion, which side should you believe? The experiment is simple. Find out for yourself! It

---

[1] S. J. Mojzsis, etc. *The RNA World*, 2nd ed. 1999, p. 7.

is obvious that a chicken egg has all the proteins necessary to form life, just as the organic soup is claimed to have had. Break an egg in a big bowl. Separate the yolk which contains less protein from the protein-rich white. Beat an eighth of the egg white into several gallons of water until it is very thin and watery, as if it had been formed in the ocean. Before you quit beating it, add a bottle of ink or food coloring to dye your protein mixture so you can see where it goes.

Now take an eye dropper and your colored protein solution, wade out into the ocean and drop one drop at a time over a large area. This will put your protein near the surface, the part of the ocean where lightning passing through the right atmosphere might have formed amino acids. It is also the depth at which waves would most effectively mix your protein into the water. Now watch to see if your protein comes together to concentrate in one spot or disperses.

If you don't have an ocean handy, you can simulate the experiment in your bathtub. Use just a drop or two of egg white. Mix it well in a quart or more of water and color it. Put one drop of the watered down protein mixture in each corner of the tub full of water, and stir to simulate the action of the waves and tides. If the protein spreads out instead of concentrating into one brightly colored spot, no first cell could ever have formed. If you have done the experiment, you just destroyed the entire sand castle of many first life theorists. You have seen for yourself that the protein does not concentrate. It spreads out.

Think about it. If any one of the steps which lead to the evolution of the first life is scientifically impossible or would not happen in practice, none of the steps following could have taken place.

Let's drop back a step to the amino acids. They too, would spread out and become more and more diluted. The same would be true for the components of DNA or RNA. No concentration, no organic broth! Something other than chemical evolution must have produced the first life. This is simple, and must have been known by the authors of textbooks which taught the exact opposite to generations of students. If they had valid arguments, why did they use this?

Some schoolbooks, recognizing that the components of cells would disperse rather than concentrate, have tried to get around the problem by claiming that the entire: "sea had the composition of 'hot dilute soup.'"[1] The ocean, however, is huge and some elements which are necessary for living things are not available in such large quantities. These, if spread throughout the ocean, would have been much too diluted to form anything. Elements like salt, and whatever else was most plentiful in the ocean at that time, whether useful or not, would have tended to predominate.

As to the next step, Dr. Susan Aldridge, published by Cambridge University Press, repeats the standard position of the optimistic group of first life advocates:

> "Once there were nucleic acids (DNA and RNA) and proteins around, however primitive, they would have tended to organize themselves into cells."[2]

---

[1]K. Arms and P. Camp, *Biology,* Holt Rinehart and Winston, 1979, p. 158.
[2]Aldridge, *The Thread of Life*, 1996, p. 82.

In her dreams! She would be one of the most famous people on earth if she could make this happen in a laboratory, even starting with perfect DNA, RNA and proteins which were bought in a chemical supply house.

She comes back down to earth a few pages later when speaking of the difficulty of finding pieces of DNA long enough to examine in an Egyptian mummy:

> "Over the course of time, DNA is degraded, as are other biomolecules such as proteins. Much of this degradation occurs shortly after death... The main feature of old DNA is that it is fragmented into small pieces..."[1]

Aldridge then says that water in liquid form (not ice or vapor) is necessary for protein production, but after proteins have been produced, they and DNA are best preserved in dry places rather than wet.

When put in oceans, lakes, etc., proteins and DNA disperse, degrade, and deteriorate rather than "organize themselves into cells." They deteriorate most rapidly when in something wet (like "organic broth").

The overly optimistic idea that by chance ever more complex chemicals built up, became concentrated in the ocean, and came together to become the first life, is scientifically impossible at every step. Why has it been taught in science classes? Was it to keep people from believing that God created? This is certainly the effect it has had on many. Undeniably, statements that are known to be false should not be taught as science in schoolbooks, no

---

[1]Aldridge, *The Thread of Life*, 1996, p. 96.

matter how important the people are who feel that the end justifies the means.

The overly optimistic idea that by chance ever more complex chemicals built up, became concentrated in the ocean, and came together to become the first life, is scientifically impossible at every step. Why has it been taught in science classes?

The belief that amino acids, proteins, the components of RNA, or whatever, became concentrated in the ocean and got together to form a cell is not belief in science, but a commitment to a particular theory about ancient history. *Science Now* quotes Orgel, one of the most important scientists doing first life research:

> "'But nailing down exactly what preceded RNA will be difficult,' Orgel says, because 'it's like any history—one can't be absolutely sure since you weren't there.'"[1]

Chemical Dilution

Sea water is not the only thing that can dilute chemicals, and render the formation of proteins and DNA impossible. Of the over 100 different amino acids which occur naturally, only 20 are commonly used to make the proteins of living things.[2] Of the chemicals produced in Miller's

---

[1]John R. Davenport, "Possible Progenitor of DNA Re-Created," *Science Now,* 11/16/2000, p. 1.
[2]"Amino Acid," *Encyclopedia Britannica CD 98.*

experiments, only 2% to 4% were amino acids of any kind. The rest were mostly tars. But assume for a moment that all of the 20 useful amino acids had been formed, and that all of these were left-handed. Even if they had not been diluted by water, they would have been diluted 96% to 98% by the non-useful chemicals produced by the same spark. Some of the chemicals needed to make proteins would not be identical to those needed for RNA and vice versa. The right ingredients for one would have diluted those for making the other.

In addition, 20 amino acids are used in making proteins and they have to be linked in the right order, so of the 20, only one would be the next to link at any one moment. The presence of all those other amino acids would make it harder to find the one in 20 which would have to link next. One reason why living cells are able to make protein is because a form of RNA called transfer RNA lines up amino acid molecules in the order in which they must be inserted into the new protein chain. This eliminates two problems:

• Including chemicals that don't belong in the protein.

• Linking the right amino acids in the wrong order.

All available evidence indicates that proteins do not form by chance. If they did form, proteins are not like amino acids which only come in 20 useful types. There are millions of possible proteins, so even if they formed and became concentrated, the ones needed for the first cell would have been hopelessly diluted by the millions of possible proteins that were not called for in that particular cell.

Coacervates

Coacervates have often been identified as a step in the evolution of the first living cell, largely because outwardly they look somewhat like cells. They are small spheres that form when some large molecules are mixed with water. If you put a little oil in some water in a clear glass container with a good lid and shake it hard you may see the very small spheres.

When coacervates are formed by heating amino acids, they are called microspheres, but more often when the term "coacervate" is used it refers to droplets of lipids (fat) in water:

> "When mixed with water, certain lipids will form a
> bubble that is called a coacervate (koh AS uhr vayt)."[1]

Because coacervates outwardly resemble cells, when microscopes were still too crude to give any idea of the complexity of cells, they became accepted as a step in the evolution of the first cell. When a coacervate breaks into two pieces, it outwardly resembles a cell dividing. Real cells split when the information in the cell commands specialized proteins called enzymes to split them in a very complex manner. Coacervates do not contain DNA or RNA, but just break apart.

Iris Fry, philosopher and science historian, in her book *The Emergence of Life on Earth,* sums up the findings of the most important first life researchers. Notice what she says about lipids (fats), the building blocks of most coacervates:

---

[1]Holt, Annotated Teacher's Edition, *Biology, Visualizing Life,* 1994, p. 202.

"Though a few organic substances–for instance certain simple amino acids–can form fairly easily under prebiotic conditions, other biochemical building blocks such as nucleotides and lipids, require for their synthesis a 'real factory.' (Cairns-Smith 1985:48). The synthesis of these substances involves a series of reactions, each reaction following the previous one in utmost accuracy."[1]

Though the lipids from which coacervates are made can only be formed by a "real factory" such as a living cell, evolutionists often claim that coacervates were a step in the spontaneous generation of the first cell:

"When mixed with water, certain lipids will form a bubble that is called a coacervate (koh AS uhr vayt)... Over millions of years, coacervates that could survive longer by taking in molecules and energy from their surroundings would have become more common than the here-today-gone-tomorrow kind. When a means arose to transfer this ability to "offspring" coacervates, probably through self-replicating RNA, life had begun."[2]

Did you notice how this textbook elevated the theory over the facts?

• There were no lipids before already living things made them.

• Coacervates are still the "here-today-gone-tomorrow kind." They have not evolved beyond that because they have neither RNA nor DNA and cannot self replicate.

---

[1]Iris Fry, *The Emergence of Life on Earth*, 2000, p. 126, 176-177.
[2]Holt, Annotated Teacher's Edition, *Biology, Visualizing Life,* 1994, p. 202.

Another high school biology book not only admits lipids do not form in nature, but adds that neither do carbohydrates, proteins, or nucleic acids (DNA and RNA):

> "Living cells are composed of four major classes of complex organic molecules: lipids, carbohydrates, proteins, and nucleic acids. Atoms do not put themselves together into these complex organic molecules on modern earth."

The solution suggested is to accept the atmosphere that Miller used in his famous experiment as that of the early earth, and infer that such an atmosphere would have resolved the problem. Miller's experiment, however, has been repeated hundreds or thousands of times and the products measured. Neither lipids, proteins, RNA, or DNA will form, not even the nucleotides from which RNA and DNA are made.

Fry's previously quoted statement that it would take "a real factory" explains why it won't work. Coacervates can be made today, but only because the lipids used were formed by real live cells!

Because I believe in heaven and hell, I am very grieved whenever I see fake science being used by our tax supported schools to convince kids that they have no Creator.

If you still believe that coacervates were a step in the evolution of life, please note that your faith, no matter how strong, is contrary to the scientific evidence. The term "coacervate" usually refers to lipids, and lipids are made by cells that already exist.

A Cell Needs a Membrane

Cells membranes have two layers which are made of lipids.[1] A cell membrane by itself is extremely thin and fragile. It would require nearly 10,000 cell membranes laid on top of one another to achieve the thickness of a sheet of paper.[2]

What does the cell's two layered membrane do?

"A living cell is a self-reproducing system of molecules held inside a container. The container is the plasma membrane—a fatty film so thin and transparent that it cannot be seen directly in the light microscope. It is simple in construction, being based on a sheet of lipid molecules... Although it serves as a barrier to prevent the contents of the cell from escaping and mixing with the surrounding medium... the plasma membrane does much more than that. Nutrients have to pass inward across it if the cell is to survive and grow, and waste products have to pass outward. Thus the membrane is penetrated by highly selective channels and pumps, formed from protein molecules, that allow specific substances to be imported while others are exported. Still other protein molecules in the membrane act as sensors to enable the cell to respond to changes in its environment."[3]

Had there been one first cell, its membrane would have

---

[1]Bruce Alberts, Dennis Bray, Alexander Johnson, Julian Lewis, Martin Raff, Keith Roberts, Peter Walter, *Essential Cell Biology, An Introduction to the Molecular Biology of the Cell,* 1998, p. 348, 363.
[2]Alberts..., *Essential Cell Biology,* 1998, p. 347-356, 363.
[3]Alberts..., *Essential Cell Biology*, 1998, p. 347.

had to do at least the things mentioned in the above quote. Without a membrane that could provide these and other essential services, a cell could not exist. A lipid membrane without the help of the protein pumps and channels lets water enter the cell, but keeps nutrients out.[1]

Which came first, a first cell that could not form without the specialized membrane holding it together and maintaining livable conditions inside, or the membrane that is only produced by a living cell? Remember, neither the lipids of cell membranes nor the proteins that make up their pumps and channels will form in nature apart from living cells.

Which came first? A first cell that could not form without the specialized membrane holding it together and maintaining livable conditions inside, or the membrane that is only produced by a living cell? Remember, neither the lipids of cell membranes nor the proteins that make up their pumps and channels will form in nature apart from living cells.

How Many Parts Does a Cell Need?

Now that we have an idea of how a cell works, I want to show that in order to function, even the simplest cell would have required a minimum number of essential parts. This is the theme of the book, *Darwin's Black Box,* by Michael Behe, associate Professor of Biochemistry at Lehigh University. Behe is not speaking of parts like arms and

---

[1]Alberts…, *Essential Cell Biology*, 1998, p. 347, 356-357.

legs, but of parts on the molecular level. He uses as an illustration the common mouse trap, the kind with a base, a wire that snaps down, etc. If even one part of a mouse trap is eliminated it will not catch a mouse. It has as few parts as it can have and still work. Behe called this *irreducible complexity* because the machine will not work if even one part is taken away. The first cell would also have needed a certain number of essential parts. All must have been present from the first, because none of these parts would work without being properly connected with the others. This is strong evidence against the idea that a cell could have been put together in a mindless fashion from an "organic broth."

Because Behe's book is devastating to the theory that the first living cell was put together by accident, many have attacked it and ridiculed both the book and Behe. However, no one has disproved it.

Just as a mouse trap will not work without all of its essential parts, a cell cannot live unless it contains a minimum number of essential parts. Most cell parts are made of specialized proteins which are formed according to instructions that the RNA brings from the DNA. Proteins, DNA, and RNA all break down fairly rapidly, so all would have to have gotten into the proposed first cell before any of them had broken down. Not even one has a long shelf life at normal temperatures.

Scientists have tried to determine how many parts the simplest cell would have needed to live. They started with the simplest one celled organism known to exist, a bacteria called Mycoplasma genitalium that can live with less parts than most bacteria because it lives in other living things.

The instruction sets in DNA are called genes. They are the basic units of heredity. Since the parts of any cell are made according to the information in its genes, the scientists knocked out one gene at a time to get a rough idea of just how simple a cell could be and still live:

> "The analysis suggests that 265 to 350 of the 480 protein-coding genes of M. genitalium are essential under laboratory growth conditions..."[1]

According to these scientists, the information necessary to build the simplest cell requires 265 to 350 genes (each of which contains the information necessary to direct the construction of one or more of the essential proteins). The minimum number of proteins usually considered necessary for cells capable of living independently (not as parasites supported by a more complex animal) are in the thousands.

Contrast this with the evolutionary speculation of how life started with a simple blob as presented by the astrobiologists who authored the book *Rare Earth:*

> "We start with a cell membrane enclosing DNA–a simple bag of protoplasm and DNA–and then evolve..."[2]

Other parts of this book, published in the year 2000, are very up to date, but to make the first life palatable, the authors revert to the simple blob. It is like referring to the most complex computer chip with many millions of transistors, etc. all wired to work together, as a simple

---

[1]*Science,* Dec. 10, 1999, Vol. 286, p. 2165.
[2]Peter D. Ward, Donald Brownlee, *Rare Earth, Why Complex Life is Uncommon in the Universe,* 2000, p. 92.

piece of resin with silica inside. The DNA, however handles millions of times as much information as a chip. Calling the first life, or something they think came before it "a simple bag of protoplasm and DNA," is simplistic.

DNA is useful only if programmed with the right information. If it were simple, scientists would be able to make a whole functioning DNA in the lab. Even if it is correctly programmed, DNA can only pass on instructions to RNA. It can't make anything itself. If "a simple bag of protoplasm and DNA" could live, scientists would have put a strand of DNA in a bag of protoplasm and made life long ago!

We can compare DNA to a computer that controls a machine in a factory. Neither the machine nor the computer can do anything without the other. Compare their "simple bag" propaganda with three true statements from another part of the same book:

> "No one has yet discovered how to combine various chemicals in a test tube and arrive at a DNA molecule."[1]

> "Some of the steps leading to the synthesis of DNA and RNA can be duplicated in the laboratory; others cannot."[2]

> "… no one has yet succeeded in creating RNA."[3]

---

[1]Peter D. Ward, Donald Brownlee, *Rare Earth, Why Complex Life is Uncommon in the Universe,* 2000, p. 62, 63, 57.
[2]Ward…, *Rare Earth...* p. 62, 63, 57.
[3]Peter D. Ward, Donald Brownlee, *Rare Earth, Why complex Life is Uncommon in the Universe,* 2000, p. 62, 63, 57.

Statements about a simple form of life coming about by chance must be understood for what they really are: Religious wishes about ancient history, not science.

If a simple bag had been formed by chance, where would it have gotten its DNA? Like a telephone, the importance of DNA is as a carrier of information. Only DNA which was already programmed with the exact information to operate that specific first cell would have worked. Where would the DNA have gone to get programmed?[1]

Not even the exterior "simple bag" could be simple. The membrane would not work, you will recall, unless it was complex enough to:

- let in the things the cell needs,

- keep out what it does not need,

- expel its waste products.

The membranes of even the simplest cells are made of lipids which we have seen "require for their synthesis a 'real factory,'" and to function must be "penetrated by highly selective channels and pumps, formed from protein molecules, that allow specific substances to be imported while others are exported."[2]

All known living things have Proteins, DNA, RNA, and a cell membrane. All of these components, with the exception of some of the simpler proteins, are too complex

---

[1] Werner Gitt, *In the Beginning Was Information*, 1997, p. 65, 67, 79, 84, 85.
[2] *Essential Cell Biology*, 1998, p. 347.

to be made in the laboratory, so the odds are highly against them having formed spontaneously in nature. Some people who realize this write me and say, "Your problem is that you just don't understand how simple the first life was."

Neither does anyone else! All known life is DNA based, though some viruses have only RNA. (Viruses are not classed as living because they depend on cells for food and reproduction.) It is true that DNA is too complex to have been generated spontaneously, but the idea (which we will examine later) that life started with a simple pre-RNA, or any other simple substance is based entirely on imagination!

Simple things, however, can be made in nature or the laboratory and experimented with much more easily than the complex ingredients of living things. Scientists have been doing experiments for years, searching for something simple that could be made to live. They have eliminated the substances that seemed most likely, but still cannot make a living thing, or even a chemical that will self replicate in a natural habitat.

Cells will not work without complex molecular machines directed by real information. This evidence points to an intelligent Creator who designed the complex cell parts which work together and provided the information to make them work. Those who instead continue to believe in a mythical simpler substance that arose with no intelligent input have chosen to embrace a faith which is contrary to the evidence and several fundamental laws of science. It is a belief system whose foundation rejects the existence of an intelligent Creator.

If you are an atheist and want to stay that way, that is your privilege. However, the evidence indicates that living things have always been:

• Composed of materials too complex to form in nature.
• Designed to work together.
• Guided by huge amounts of information.

If, on the other hand, you are not an atheist, why should you follow their leap of faith in the impossible? Kids in tax supported public schools should not be taught that it is scientific to believe that life started when RNA, DNA, and proteins got together inside a membrane. It is not scientific because it is contrary to the evidence.

People have protested to me: "In the future researchers may find evidence that supports a naturalistic origin of life." This only underlines the fact that their faith is contrary to the evidence which is now available.

So what are the bare essentials of the simplest cell? At the very least it would need:

• The information necessary to build the cell.
• A container for the information (DNA and/or RNA).
• The materials which DNA must have at hand to do the work of making the cell (left-handed amino acids, ribosomes, proteins, and other components).
• The essential minimum number of molecular machines that do much of the work of the cell. What good would half made ribosomes be that could not yet make proteins? About as useful as bumble bees that had only evolved one third of the wing surface needed to fly!
• A way to get the necessary information from the DNA to the parts which do the work of the cell.

• A source of energy as well as something that converts this energy to a usable form.

• A membrane that will hold the cell's parts together while letting the materials the cell needs pass in, and its waste products out.

• Life! Think about it. Right after dying, many dead cells still contain the necessary parts, but they are dead cells, not living cells.

All known cells are constructed in such a way that no one part by itself can make any of its proteins, the DNA, the RNA, or the external membrane that a cell must have. Therefore, no known cell can function without at least some minimum number of simultaneously existing parts, each designed to work with the others.

The belief that some primitive ancestor to the cell could do this in the past is not based on observation or having repeated the process in the lab. It may be part of a philosophic belief system, a religion, or an opinion about ancient history, but science it is not!

Getting the Parts Together

We have seen that the simplest cell known needs at least a few hundred parts. These parts are too complex to form without intelligent instructions. In addition, once formed they break down rapidly.

Now we are ready to move on to the next fatal flaw in the theory of the chance formation of the first life: The parts would have had to get together. The cell would not work if the DNA were floating in the China Sea, while the proteins were in the Mediterranean and the membrane which was to enclose them was in the Atlantic off the New England coast.

If even one of the hundreds of really necessary proteins had not been together with the RNA and the pre-programmed DNA inside that microscopically small cell membrane, a functioning cell would not have formed. To make the lucky accident even less plausible, all the parts would have to have gotten together inside that cell membrane at about the same time, before even one essential part had broken down.

Forget the good old days and the bad old microscopes. Calling a cell a simple blob or a "simple bag of protoplasm and DNA" may be a useful ploy to manipulate minds, but in the real world, cells are composed of many parts that work together. Even if something was able to form RNA, DNA, and the hundreds of proteins necessary to form the first cell, they could only have become part of the cell if they were all in the same spot at the same time inside a microscopically tiny cell membrane. If you still believe all this happened with no Creator to direct the project, please recognize that it does not happen in nature or even in the laboratory, so the evidence and the odds are very strongly against it. Those who believe it do so because of faith in a teacher, a book, or a religious viewpoint.

Spontaneous Generation Doesn't Happen

It was once believed that life just came about. Rats were generated by piles of old rags, maggots by meat, etc. Many felt the Bible's teaching that God long ago created living things that brought forth according to their kind was naive and pre-scientific. They thought that they possessed a higher, more advanced knowledge. Actually they believed in pre-scientific fables which were laid to rest by the famous experiments of Louis Pasteur in 1860. By boiling and then maintaining sterile conditions, Pasteur established the Principle of Biogenesis: living things come only from living things, spontaneous generation does not happen. It is a foundational principle of biology, upon which much of today's food preservation industry is based.

Many today, however, believe this principle of science must have been circumvented to permit the evolution of the first life. They usually avoid the term "spontaneous generation," since everyone knows that spontaneous generation cannot happen, and use the word "abiogenesis" instead. Why use a term that might prejudice people against the idea that life spontaneously arose from chemicals?

Two schoolbooks I found admit that what was being proposed was spontaneous generation. One claimed it could happen in the past because the atmosphere was different. The other because the environment was different. Scientists, however, have tried many different atmospheres and environments. Life does not form! Not only do rats not come from rags, a living cell has never arisen from any mixture of amino acids; or even from perfectly formed DNA, RNA, and proteins. When kids are taught the opposite, they should also be informed that what they are being taught is an opinion about what happened in prehistoric times. It is not supported by evidence, and is contrary to the most basic laws and principles of science.

Lets look at some specific problems with the idea of spontaneous generation, and the attempts that have been made to provide solutions.

Problem
Oxygen in the air is very active chemically. Chemicals claimed to have combined with each other to form protein, DNA, and RNA would have combined with the oxygen instead.

The proposed solution
The atmosphere was different than today, and did not contain oxygen.

First problem with the proposed solution
"But many researchers now hold that the ancient Earth's atmosphere, compared with the earlier view, had more oxygen and less hydrogen—as the atmosphere does today."[1]

"It was puzzling, but geologists know from their analyses of the oldest known rocks that the oxygen level of the early atmosphere had to be much higher than previously calculated. Analyses of these rocks, estimated to be more than 3.5 billion years old, found oxidized iron in amounts that called for atmospheric oxygen levels to be at least 110 times greater, and perhaps up to one billion times greater than otherwise accepted."[2]

----

[1]Gorman, Jessica, "Cosmic Chemistry Gets Creative." *Science News,* 05/19/2001, Vol. 159, Issue 20, p. 318.

[2]"New Evidence on Evolution of Early Atmosphere and Life," *Bulletin of the American Meteorological Society,* Vol. 63, Nov. 1982, p. 1329; see also: Clemmey and Badham, "Oxygen in the Precambrian Atmosphere: An Evaluation of the Geological Evidence," *Geology,* Vol. 10, March 1982, pp. 141, 145.

Second problem with the proposed solution

Life could not exist on earth if it not for a protective layer of ozone, a form of oxygen in the stratosphere which shields us from the harmful ultraviolet rays. The ozone layer is formed from oxygen in the air. If there had been no oxygen in the atmosphere, there would have been no ozone, and without the ozone, any life that began would have been killed by ultraviolet rays.

Proposed solution

The first life formed deep enough in the ocean so the water would shield it from the ultraviolet rays.

Life on earth could not exist if it were not for a protective layer of ozone, a form of oxygen in the stratosphere which shields us from the harmful ultraviolet rays. The ozone layer is formed from oxygen in the air. If there had been no oxygen in the atmosphere, there would have been no ozone, and without the ozone, any life that began would have been killed by ultraviolet rays.

Problem

Any amino acids in the ocean would spread out rather than concentrating and could never have gotten together to form proteins.

Solution

Life began in a shallow lagoon or a puddle where evaporation concentrated the chemicals into an organic broth.

Problems with the solution

• The warmer temperature of the water in a lagoon or puddle leads to the rapid breakdown of amino acids, RNA, DNA, and proteins. It has to do with the Second Law of Thermodynamics.

• If life had formed in a shallow lagoon, ultraviolet rays would have killed it.

Solution

The first cell formed in water deep within the earth or in a deep sea vent where hot water wells up out of the earth.

Problem

Water from these locations is very hot, so the entropy of the Second Law of Thermodynamics kicks in with a vengeance. While some living cells get along just fine in hot water, their components RNA, DNA, and proteins break down in minutes or hours outside of a cell. They are only protected inside some living cells. No concentration of these materials could possibly have built up.

Another problem

RNA and DNA will not form outside already living cells. If they did in the prehistoric past as is claimed, they would have to have been formed already programmed to direct the formation of each of the specific proteins needed by the first cell.

Solution

RNA formed on clay. The molecular structure of the clay served as a template to build the RNA molecule.

Problems

Clay does not have the same molecular structure as RNA, and will not serve as a template to form RNA. In addition, the purpose of RNA is to carry information. To be anything other than a microscopic speck of goo, RNA would have needed very specific information not contained in clay.

Life only comes from life. This is a basic principle of science, the Principle of Biogenesis. The unscientific belief that the first living cell must have been an exception to that principle is based only on faith and is contrary to the evidence.

Conclusion

No matter what evolutionary proposal one might be tempted to accept, spontaneous generation never happens, not even in a sophisticated laboratory and no matter what oxygen-free atmosphere is tried. In fact, not even one of the hundreds of necessary proteins has ever been known to form outside of a living cell in conditions that might exist in nature. Why? *Life only comes from life.* This is a basic principle of science, the Principle of Biogenesis. The unscientific belief that the first living cell must have been an exception to that principle is based only on faith and is contrary to the evidence.

If spontaneous generation (or abiogenesis as its proponents prefer to call it) must be taught in schools supported by the taxes of those who do not believe in it, would it not be more honest to teach it as philosophy, or an opinion about an unobserved event in history, rather than as science?

3

The Cell's Information

Proteins Are Folded to Fit

As soon as a new protein molecule is made, while it is moving into its place in the cell, it folds into the right shape to connect and work with the proteins next to it. Some use the illustration of a hand in a glove to describe how a protein must fit. Others liken it to the way a key fits in a lock. Here is how it works:

> "Comprising strings of amino acids that are joined like links of a chain, proteins fold into a highly complex, three-dimensional shape that determines their function. Any change in shape dramatically alters the function of a protein, and even the slightest change in the folding process can turn a desirable protein into a disease."[1]

A number of scientists had a contest to see who would be first to come up with a computer model showing how to

[1]www.no.ibm.com/nyheter/des99/bluegene.html

fold a protein correctly so it would fit with the neighboring proteins and function properly.

The next year they came together to see who had devised the best solution. The headline of the article in the Portland *Oregonian* was "Cell Wins, Scientists Lose." The conference decided that even with the computers we have now, it would take billions of years to solve this problem that the cell solves in a few seconds (a few minutes for the more complex proteins). About a year later, on December 6, 1999, IBM announced it was building the world's most powerful super computer to tackle the gene folding problem:

> "The machine, dubbed Blue Gene, will be turned loose on a single problem. The computer will try to model the way a human protein folds into a particular shape that gives it its unique biological properties."[1]

It is because of the need for computational power to figure out how proteins fold that I have placed protein folding in the chapter on information.

The argument has been made that the composition of the protein determines the way it will fold. This is sometimes true, but if it were always true, there would be no need for a super computer to figure out how to fold them.

Specialized proteins called *chaperones* or chaperonins, have recently been discovered which move newly made proteins along to the places where they must fit with other proteins. On the way, they help them fold correctly and help fit them into their place. But what makes the

[1]Justin Gillis, *The Sunday Oregonian*, June 4, 2000, A5.

chaperones themselves fold correctly? They too have chaperones.

Because our top scientists cannot yet fold proteins properly, few of the simple proteins which they can make in the world's most expensive laboratories will work in living things. Though they may be the same chemically, unless they fold correctly, they might as well be miniature spaghetti as far as biological activity is concerned!

Having understood the importance of a protein's shape, you can get a better grasp of an important concept that we have already studied. If a right-handed amino acid molecule is included among the all left-handed ones, a protein's shape is changed and it won't work. It's like a piece of a puzzle turned upside down with the bump sticking out on the wrong side. No matter how it folds, it will not attach correctly to the proteins around it.

Many believe that in the past, proteins formed spontaneously, fit together and functioned. This belief is probably held over from a time when the difficulties of protein folding were unknown.

Addressing Proteins

When a protein is folded to fit so it will function correctly with the proteins next to it, it will only fit in one spot in the cell. How does it find its place?

> "In the 1970's Blobel and his colleagues began pondering how proteins know their correct locations within cells. Even though proteins are confronted with billions of possibilities, they always know where to go. How?

> An equivalent task would be to hover above a vast

city – say, five times larger than New York – and then be able to whiz straight down to a tiny house on a tiny street somewhere in the middle of it."[1]

In 1999, "The Nobel Prize for Medicine went to Dr. Guenter Blobel of The Rockefeller University in New York"[2] for discovering the amino acid address tags that direct each protein to its proper place in the cell.

"He worked out the molecular details of how each signal is processed, and showed that the processes are universal, operating similarly in animal, plant, and yeast cells."[3]

The first cell could not function without a way to make proteins, fold them correctly, and attach address tags. Proteins made in the lab will not work until scientists master the problems of folding and addressing.

Turning off Proteins

For a cell to work, it is not enough for its proteins to be folded correctly and be sent to the right places. The cell must also have the right amount of each protein. Therefore, protein production must be turned on and off at the right times.[4] If a ribosome kept making more and more copies of any given protein, it would completely use up many of its raw materials. It's like the difference between burning the right amount of wood in your fireplace, and burning down

---

1. Web link no longer available.

[2] www4.cnn.com/HEALTH/9910/11/nobel.medicine.03/index.html

[3] "Dr. George Johnson on Science," *St. Louis Post Dispatch,* http://www.txtwriter.com/Onscience/Articles/Nobel.html

[4] Susan Aldridge, *The Thread of Life, The Story of Genes and Genetic Engineering,* Cambridge University Press, 1996, p. 47-53.

the whole house. Also, if there was even one protein that the cell could not stop making after it had made enough, that cell would eventually be jammed so full of that protein it would die. If abiogenesis made the first cell, unless it included a control system, the new cell would have died after it started making the first protein and was unable to turn off the production when it had enough.

If a hypothetical first cell had been made, the initial quantities of each of its essential ingredients would have to have been close to perfect, and then kept that way. How could it have worked if it had been crammed full of:
- The proteins which were easiest to make?
- Any proteins at all whose production the cell was not yet programmed to turn off?
- Any proteins not called for in its program?
- Other unwanted chemicals?

The cell has a number of ways of turning protein production on or off. One is for a specific enzyme to attach itself to a spot on the protein. The enzyme may be very small, but it changes the shape of the protein a little bit, so it no longer fits precisely with the proteins around it.[1] This makes it biologically inactive just as it would have been had it included a right-handed amino acid, or had it been folded improperly.

One of the most important methods of turning on or off protein production is by means of regulatory DNA sequences. They are specific stretches of DNA whose job is to tell the cell when to start and stop the production of a

---

[1]Susan Aldridge, *The Thread of Life...* 1996, p. 47-53.

protein. However, the DNA cannot turn protein production on or off by itself. Each sequence works with a specific gene regulatory protein. The regulatory protein folds perfectly to fit the correct spot on the DNA, and work with it. Together, DNA and protein form a miniature control system; a switch that turns the correct gene or genes on or off at the right times.[1]

Neither the regulatory DNA sequences nor the regulatory proteins will work without the other, so it would seem that both should have been discarded by natural selection unless they both came into being perfectly coordinated at the moment the life of the cell began. At that same moment, of course, each regulatory protein also needed a fully functioning tag that would send it to the exact spot on the DNA where it would fit and function. On the way, it had to be folded correctly so it would fit when it got there. All must be in place for a cell to work.

Obviously, if the new cell did not have a functioning membrane in place at the same time, all these complex parts would just be loose goo floating away into the ocean. I ask atheists and agnostics, is your faith big enough to believe that all these complex substances that a cell requires to work, and the information to run them, just happened to come about at the same time with no Creator involved?

The RNA World

Stanley Miller became famous because of his experiment in 1953 which produced amino acids. It was

---

[1]Alberts…, *Essential Cell Biology*, 1998, p. 259-262.

imagined that amino acids would combine to form proteins which would get together with DNA to form the first cell. However, amino acids do not combine spontaneously to form proteins. Not even Miller accepts this idea today. In addition, DNA does not form outside of cells, not even in the laboratory. Some readers may still believe life formed because amino acids got together and made proteins, but Miller does not.

No one was there to see life form, so Miller and others have weighed the evidence, and have become convinced that amino acids do not get together to form proteins, nor does DNA form outside of already living cells and then get together with the proteins inside a cell membrane.

Because of that, Miller and many others now follow another suggested solution to the origin of life. They believe that RNA or a proposed simple forerunner of RNA, which is referred to as *pre-RNA*, must have been the key to the spontaneous generation of life. This idea is called the RNA world. Many scientists are now searching for evidence to substantiate this idea.

How Did Theorizing about the RNA World Begin?

Because viruses are simpler than cells, some people once thought a virus might have been the first form of life. The idea was dropped because viruses can't live independently. They depend on cells for both nutrition and reproduction. It had been noticed, however, that some viruses only have RNA, a simpler system than that of cells, which have both DNA and RNA. This led to the idea that the precursor to the first cell might have been RNA.

Since RNA would be even more difficult to produce by chance than protein, many imagine there must have been a forerunner to RNA. They propose a simpler self-replicating material which they call pre-RNA. They believe it eventually evolved into what they call a simple RNA, which they believe had many of the properties of both RNA and DNA. Theorists believe that, like DNA, this simple substance contained all the cell's information and could make copies of itself. In addition, they believe the imagined simple substance could catalyze chemical reactions (make the reactions take place) much better than real RNA; well enough to produce proteins all by itself.

Why Abandon Proteins for RNA?

Here is the reason according to one schoolbook:

> "Scientists have not been able to cause amino acids dissolved in water to join together to form proteins. The energy-requiring chemical reactions that join amino acids are reversible and do not occur spontaneously in water. However, most scientists no longer argue that the first proteins assembled spontaneously. Instead, they now propose that the initial macromolecules were composed of RNA, and that RNA later catalyzed the formation of proteins."[1]

This is a very significant admission. For the last two or three generations schoolbooks championed the belief that life began when protein and DNA were formed by chance in organic broth and got together. Since the evidence

---

[1]George B. Johnson, Peter H. Raven, *Biology, Principles & Explorations,* Holt, Rinehart and Winston, 1996 p. 235.

against this idea was generally not mentioned, some of you will have trouble believing that the protein-to-life idea was not right. What scientific evidence was offered for the amino acid to protein to living cell idea? Other than the first step, the formation of amino acids, to the best of my knowledge, there never was any. Now even schoolbooks agree that amino acids getting together to form proteins is false, even though it was taught to two generations.

While looking through some old books, I found one written by a creationist scientist in 1976 which discussed the same problem and came to the same conclusion as the schoolbook quoted above: proteins won't form in water.[1] For many of the years that students were being turned away from their Creator by the idea that amino acids spontaneously produced proteins and got together with DNA to form the first cell, good evidence already existed that it was scientifically impossible.

I rejoice that the schoolbook quoted on the previous page now clearly admits that amino acids won't join together in water to form proteins but I am saddened that it fails to mention the fact that neither RNA (nor even the nucleotides of which RNA is made) will form in water either:

> "…water greatly interferes with the linking of amino acids and nucleotides into chains, a crucial step in the origin of life. "[2]

Did any real evidence exist for life having been formed without a Creator? If it did, why did the books claim that

---

[1]James F. Coppedge, *Evolution: Possible or Impossible?* 1976, p. 107.
[2]Iris Fry, *The Emergence of Life on Earth*, 2000, p. 184. See also p. 245, quoted from Chyba 1998:17.

proteins formed in water, and got together with DNA to form life, when the evidence was strongly against this claim?

Many of you have seen this book on *www.creationism.org* as I was writing it, and have answered that the spontaneous formation of life is science, while what I believe is just religion. One person recently upheld the old argument that amino acids formed in nature would unite to form proteins which would get together with DNA to form a cell. He told me this was based on scientific observation and experimentation and could be verified. He said that what I believe is not scientific, but this is.

Clearly no one was there to observe how life was formed, so the idea that proteins formed in organic broth was not based on observation. The experimental evidence is strongly against the idea, as the correct amino acids have been put together in an organic broth many times, but no proteins will ever form. Most scientists are now convinced that life could not have started that way. Obviously the idea is not scientific, but he and millions of others are convinced it is. One of my goals in this book is to give a bit of balance in evaluating the evidence.

The scientific evidence overwhelmingly indicates that proteins will not form in nature. The schoolbook said that scientists "now propose that the initial macromolecules were composed of RNA," But the evidence is even stronger that RNA will not form outside of living cells. In addition, in order for life to begin in this way, before the first RNA decomposed it would have needed to produce other RNA (called "self replicating RNA"). No self replicating RNA has been found, and laboratories are not capable of making any, so those who will not accept a Creator are searching for a simple self replicating pre-RNA which could have evolved to a living cell.

So far, their experiments have failed to form any pre-RNA that will self replicate without continuing input from the scientist, but the search continues.

Davenport, a scientist with another theory evaluates the evidence for the RNA world:

> "But where the first RNA came from is a mystery; it's hard to see how the chemicals on early Earth could have combined to form the complicated nucleotides that make up RNA."[1]

Davenport believes the evidence is against even the nucleotides of RNA or pre-RNA having been produced by a naturalistic method. He tells it like it is, because he has another idea. He suggests that life came from another chemical which would be easier to form. Since RNA, DNA, and proteins do exist in all living things, somewhere in the process, a great number of proteins and RNA would have to have formed many coordinated complex molecular machines. These machines would not work unless all their essential parts became present and assembled at the same time. Functional molecular machines do not just pop up. DNA contains the complex information that puts them together and makes them work. There is no real evidence that DNA was ever produced by RNA, as the RNA world

---

[1] John R. Davenport, "Possible Progenitor of DNA Re-Created," *Science Now,* 11/16/2000, p. 1.

proponents conclude, but had it been, it would have to have been programmed with all the necessary information to direct that specific cell. Did it get its program from RNA? Then where did RNA get it? No evidence exists that either matter or energy can produce meaningful information. The information that runs the cell must have been produced by an intelligent source.

To Believe or Not to Believe

Most atheists and agnostics hold their belief, at least in part, from having been taught that life resulted from proteins forming spontaneously in the ocean. Many were convinced that this was true science while the belief that God created life was unscientific. Now even schoolbooks admit that proteins won't form in water. If this is you, where will you now place your faith?

• In the RNA world, even though there is no evidence supporting it?

• In an intelligent Creator who could create both the materials and the information that directs them?

Many have accepted atheism or agnosticism as their religion, and defend it no matter how contrary it is to the evidence. Many of these folks are now reluctantly abandoning proteins and following the crowd to place their trust in the spontaneous generation of RNA. Some who before would have condemned as unscientific my skepticism of the protein to cell idea, have switched, and now write emails saying, "The RNA world is scientific fact. What the creationists believe is religion. Creationists hold to a religious faith. I am scientific." There is, however, no scientific evidence that a self replicating pre-

RNA ever existed, nor can any be formed in the laboratory which will self replicate in a natural setting. Even if it could, the primary function of RNA is to contain information. The evidence indicates that the substances that hold information were made by the intelligence that gave them the information. They could not have survived without it.

Could it Happen?

After many years of trying in many laboratories, no one has been able to produce a satisfactory pre-RNA, and there is no evidence that any ever existed. In spite of that, Miller and many others have faith that it must have existed.

Even though the evidence is against the idea, textbooks today teach that life was started by RNA, just as older books taught that amino acid spontaneously formed protein which, together with the other essential ingredients, formed a cell. Some textbooks go so far as to use Miller's old experiment which produced amino acid to make the spontaneous origin of RNA sound easy and assured:

"First, RNA nucleotides formed from simple gas molecules in much the same way as in experiments similar to those done by Miller and Urey. Nucleotides then assembled spontaneously into small chains... These small chains were able to make copies of themselves. Once replicating molecules like these appear, natural selection and evolution are possible."[1]

It sounds scientific as you read it, but I cannot find one honest fact in the whole statement. Can you? Scientists

[1]Holt, Annotated Teacher's Edition, *Biology, Visualizing Life,* 1994, p. 201.

have repeated the experiment many times since Miller, and in many variations. Some of the bases which nucleotides contain were formed, but no nucleotides. Though nucleotides break down spontaneously, they do not form from simple gas molecules, so they do not assemble spontaneously into small chains which can make copies of themselves. Neither RNA nor DNA can even be made in the lab.[1]

John Horgan, writing to a more scientific audience, is a little bit more up front about the difficulty of assembling RNA:

> "RNA and its components are difficult to synthesize in a laboratory under the best of conditions, much less under plausible prebiotic ones."[2]

Orgel, one of the most important first life researchers, speaks of the problems:

> "There were no chemical supply houses in the primitive earth. What's more, even if the ingredients had been present, the chemical steps needed to assemble them would have been difficult, if not impossible in the prebiotic world."[3]

Two astrobiologists take the admission of difficulty a step farther:

---

[1]Peter D. Ward, Donald Brownlee, *Rare Earth, Why Complex Life is Uncommon in the Universe,* 2000, p. 62, 63.
[2]John Horgan, "In the Beginning," *Scientific American,* Vol. 264, Feb. 1991, p. 119.
[3]Jon Cohen, "Novel Center Seeks to Add Spark to Origins of Life," *Science*, Vol. 270, Dec. 22, 1995, p. 1926.

"The abiotic synthesis of RNA remains the most enigmatic step in the evolution of the first life, for no one has yet succeeded in creating RNA."[1]

("Abiotic synthesis of RNA," means making it outside of an already living cell).

Fry goes a step farther, and admits that not even the building blocks that make up RNA (nucleotides) are ever produced in nature outside of real live cells. Remember this quote from the section on coacervates?

"...other biochemical building blocks such as nucleotides and lipids, require for their synthesis a 'real factory.' ...The synthesis of these substances involves a series of reactions, each reaction following the previous one in utmost accuracy."[2]

To make the formation of RNA or the theorized pre-RNA even more difficult, the presence of,

"...water greatly interferes with the linking of amino acids and nucleotides into chains, a crucial step in the origin of life."[3]

It gets worse! Remember that proteins will not function unless their amino acids are all left-handed? RNA and DNA will not work unless the sugars in their building blocks are exclusively right-handed:

"all sugars in the backbones of DNA and RNA are of the D, or right-handed type... copying can be

---

[1]Peter D. Ward, Donald Brownlee, *Rare Earth, Why Complex Life is Uncommon in the Universe*, 2000, p. 57; See also p. xix, 60, 63-64.
[2]Iris Fry, *The Emergence of Life on Earth,* 2000, p. 126, 176-177.
[3]Iris Fry, *The Emergence of Life on Earth,* 2000, p. 245.

achieved only when all the nucleotides are of the right-handed type."[1]

In real life only already living cells are capable of producing all right-handed sugars. Sugars produced in nature are half right-handed and half left-handed, and could not have contributed to the formation of functional pre-RNA. Made up stories to the contrary are based on faith alone, and are contrary to the evidence.

Books that make RNA formation sound easy are simply not telling the truth. The problems in RNA formation are so numerous and so serious that many scientists are now searching for a more simple solution.[2]

Books that make RNA formation sound easy are simply not telling the truth. The problems in RNA formation are so numerous and so serious that many scientists are now searching for a more simple solution.

Most scientists, even those who do not believe there was a Creator, if pressed, must agree that both proteins and RNA are too complex to have been generated spontaneously. Because of this, many of them are searching for another way that life could have started. At the moment, many favor one of three proposed solutions which some believe might be possible. They defend their position by explaining why the other two would not work:

---

[1] Iris Fry, *The Emergence of Life on Earth,* 2000, p. 143-144.
[2] Iris Fry, *The Emergence of Life on Earth,* 2000, p. 142-145.

• Many are looking for a simplified RNA, something which contains information but also has the ability to self replicate, something known RNA can't do.

• Others, turning back toward the older protein solution, are trying to find a simpler substance that may have led up to proteins. They believe that the first steps toward life were chemicals that did not carry information.

• Still others find both solutions impossible, and are hoping to find life on another planet from which a living cell could somehow have come to earth.

Those of you who do not believe that God created life, have, for the most part, based your opinion, not on the idea of an RNA world, but on faith in the claim that life formed after amino acids had linked together to form proteins which then got together with DNA to form cells. Based on the evidence that in nature, amino acids do not link together to form proteins, the majority of evolutionists are now calling you to shift your faith to RNA[1] which is even harder to form than protein.

Replication and Catalysis

"So far no RNA molecules that direct the replication of other RNA molecules have been identified in nature."[2]

Have scientists been able to construct self replicating RNA?

---

[1]Steven A. Brenner, etc. *The RNA World,* 2nd ed. 1999, p. 163.
[2]Leslie E. Orgel, "The Origin of Life on Earth," *Scientific American*, Vol. 271, Oct. 1994, p. 78.

"RNA can make new copies of itself only with a great deal of help from the scientist…"[1]

Speculation about RNA replicating itself in nature is just that: speculation! DNA can reproduce because it comes in two identical strands that are separated with the help of proteins at the moment of reproduction. Then, with the help of other specialized proteins, each strand replaces its missing half using the half it still has as a template. RNA, on the other hand, is made by copying the information which is already "written" on short portions of a cell's DNA. This process requires the assistance of proteins, and RNA is normally a single strand which would be harder to replicate than a double strand like DNA which splits apart to reproduce.

If, however, self replicating pre-RNA could be formed, it would have to be programmed before it could function. It would be like a computer whose hard drive had no system and no program.

The questions remain:
• How could RNA or the proposed pre-RNA be formed outside of a cell? Remember how Wald grappled with the problem of how the production of living things would require a miracle, and suggested that two billion years were time enough to perform miracles? Others have also grappled with the problem that the evidence makes it quite

---

[1]John Horgan, "In the Beginning," *Scientific American,* Vol. 264, Feb. 1991, p. 119.

clear that what is being asked for is scientifically impossible, and have tried to pull some other naturalistic miracle out of their hats. Some have suggested that clay or fool's gold would have served as a template to produce the first pre-RNA. Scientists have experimented with these substances to no avail. If, however, self replicating pre-RNA could be formed, it would have to be programmed before it could function. It would be like a computer whose hard drive had no system and no program. No clay template exists which could program pre-RNA to self replicate or to catalyze the chemical reactions that produce proteins. If one accepts the clay template idea, the question is no longer, "who programmed the pre-RNA?" It becomes, "who programmed the clay (or the fool's gold) which programmed the pre-RNA?" At whatever stage the programming was done, intelligence was required.

If pre-RNA did come about in some spontaneous way, unless it came into being already programmed with the correct information for making each necessary protein sequence, it would be of no more use in making proteins than a book of instructions with blank pages.

The purpose of DNA and RNA is to contain and pass on large quantities of complex information. Without the information, neither RNA nor the suggested pre-RNA, nor DNA would be of any use at all. The first part of the name "fool's gold" suggests the quality of the information clay or fool's gold would have been able to pass on to pre-RNA. Neither clay nor fool's gold can be forced to produce in the laboratory a pre-RNA which will self replicate in nature. Why should you have faith that outside of the lab, where it would have been much more difficult, they made pre-RNA, and passed on the instructions which enabled it to reproduce? The evidence is against it. Clay has no such information to pass on. If you choose to believe in clay as the programmer of life, you must believe it in spite of the evidence, not because of it. If you do not want to believe that God could create life, you can believe that clay did. You must believe in more or less the same miracle, but you can remain an atheist.

If pre-RNA could self replicate, when it evolved into real RNA it would have had to loose that ability because real RNA is not self-replicating. It is produced by copying information from a short section of DNA.

Top RNA world scientist Leslie Orgel noted that pre-RNA would have needed:

> "...two properties not evident today, a capacity to replicate without the help of proteins, and an ability to catalyze each step of protein synthesis."[1]

In nature, even DNA cannot replicate without the help of a good number of specialized proteins called enzymes. The enzymes divide the DNA into two strands, then make each strand into a complete DNA. DNA directs the making of RNA and furnishes its information. Orgel is saying that if RNA or a more simple pre-RNA came before DNA, it would have had to:

---

[1]Leslie E. Orgel, "The Origin of Life on Earth," *Scientific American,* Vol. 271, Oct. 1994, p. 78.

• Make copies of itself from the very beginning, and to have done so without any help from enzymes, a trick that neither DNA nor real RNA can perform.

• "Catalyze each step of protein synthesis." RNA can only catalyze a few of the steps with limited effectiveness. Enzymes are much more efficient at making chemical reactions happen than is RNA.

> "Enzymes speed up reactions, often by a factor or a million or more... that is, they act as catalysts that permit cells to make or break covalent bonds at will... making life possible... Each type of enzyme is highly specific, catalyzing only a specific type of reaction."[1]

> "It is now generally accepted among biological scientists that for every biological reaction that has been discovered, there is, and for all those to be discovered in the future there will be, a specific catalyst to perform the task."[2]

The imagined primitive pre-RNA would have had to catalyze not just one specific biological reaction as does each enzyme, but all of the reactions essential to life.

According to the RNA world hypothesis, enzymes would not have come into being until RNA had made them. In real life, DNA contains the information necessary to link in their correct order the amino acids to make each protein, including those that are to form the enzymes. If

---

[1] Alberts..., *Essential Cell Biology*, 1998, p. 348, 363.
[2] E. J. Shew, R. A. Lindsey, R. V. Blander, *Lamarck's Signature, How Retrogenes Are Changing Darwin's Natural Selection Paradigm*, 1998, p. 36-37.

pre-RNA did come about in some spontaneous way, unless it came into being already programmed with the correct information for making each necessary protein sequence, it would be of no more use in making proteins than a book of instructions with blank pages.

Some kinds of RNA in living cells do have a limited ability to catalyze chemical reactions; that is, they can make some reactions happen. For example, because it receives the instructions from the DNA, one kind of RNA can cut the DNA strand. This is often used to imply that the suggested primitive pre-RNA could have made all of the proteins a cell must have to live. This is like bragging that since your husband can pick up a heavy sledgehammer, his grandfather could lift the Empire State Building. The fact that RNA can function a little bit as a catalyst is certainly no guarantee that a more primitive pre-RNA could, with no help from DNA, catalyze a lot.[1]

Here is a recent high school textbook explanation:

> "Perhaps RNA was the first self-replicating information-storage molecule. After it had formed, it could also have catalyzed the assembly of the first proteins…"[2]

Perhaps if one could believe the first step he could also believe the second, but both steps must be taken by pure blind faith! RNA in nature can neither self replicate, nor catalyze the assembly of proteins, and years of research

---

[1]S. E. Benner et al. *The RNA World,* 2nd ed. 1999, p. 165-166.
[2]George B. Johnson, Peter H. Raven, *Biology, Principles & Explorations,* Holt, Rinehart and Winston, 1996, p. 230.

have not been able to give it those abilities. It would be just as scientific to say, "After it had formed, it could also jump over the moon."

Benner mentions another problem:

> "Curiously, catalysis on the one hand and information storage on the other, place competing and contradictory demands on molecular structure that make a single molecule that does both difficult to find."[1]

If there was a pre-RNA which was a whiz bang protein assembler, we would be faced with another problem. The number of useful proteins is much smaller than the huge number of proteins which would have been of no use at all. Did a mind guide the proposed pre-RNA to make just the right proteins? If not, and pre-RNA made proteins as they happened to come, Brig Clyce calculates that one protein in every ten to the 500th power would have been a possibly useful protein. If every cubic quarter inch of ocean produced 100 billion trials a minute, it would take hundreds of times longer than the 4.6 billion years which many believe to be the age of the earth, just to produce the first useful protein. Not just one, but at least hundreds of different useful proteins would have been needed. These would have to fold, fit, and function together.

In the time available, there is no way pre-RNA could have happened upon just the specific proteins that would be needed later in the first cell.[2]

---

[1] S. A. Benner et al. *The RNA World*, 2nd ed. 1999, p. 173.
[2] Brig Clyce Cosmic Ancestry, www.panspermia.org/rnaworld.htm

Natural Selection

Many atheists are becoming convinced that chance could never have produced proteins, DNA, nor RNA, so they are speculating it was done by natural selection.

At best, natural selection, the executioner of the unfit, eliminates organisms which are less able to live and reproduce, so the more fit survive to leave descendants. *Some evolutionists,* however, *credit it with a creative ability* and speculate that it did not just work on living things. In their imagination, they are pushing the effects of natural selection back from living things to ever more simple chemicals, and changing its function from weeding out the unfit to creating. They, like Wald, have seen the enormity of the evidence against the spontaneous formation of the complex chemicals of living things, and have searched for something that would provide the needed miracle.

The natural selection they are suggesting is not normal natural selection, but an imaginary natural selection that steps in and performs miracles when needed. Normal natural selection, if it applied to chemicals, it would favor those that are formed most easily, and those which break down most slowly. It would not have selected the many complex, extremely hard to form chemicals that would be needed to do a particular job in the future. RNA, DNA, proteins, and lipids are extremely difficult to form, and once formed, break down quite rapidly in the presence of water or heat. None form in nature, and most cannot even be made in the lab. If natural selection really did work on a chemical level, it would not choose these chemicals.

Real natural selection does not work on chemicals because chemicals cannot reproduce, so any chemical which was selected could not reproduce itself. The next chemical to pop up might be completely different. *Natural selection works on organisms which have an information storage system,* and are able to reproduce copies of themselves, after their own kind, but with some variation within the kind. Then, when the inferior ones are eliminated, those which remain continue to make copies of themselves.

Many evolutionists understand this and insist it was only after a self replicating information system was in place that natural selection could have begun. Otherwise there would have been no way to maintain any advances which might have been made. Chemicals put together by the random forces of nature are random, except that those easiest to produce are produced in greater numbers, and the very difficult are not produced at all.

If various self replicating pre-RNAs already existed, natural selection may or may not have been able to select the one that happened to reproduce itself better than the others, but it certainly could not invent or create the first pre-RNA, or empower pre-RNA to invent proteins. (The proposed pre-RNA is not protein but nucleic acid like RNA and DNA).

If pre-RNA could put together a protein capable of functioning as an enzyme, until that enzyme had been perfected enough to catalyze some needed reaction better than the pre-RNA itself, natural selection would eliminate the enzyme in favor of the catalyzing ability of the pre-

RNA. The more successful pre-RNA might have been in accomplishing enzyme like activities, the more likely it would have been for natural selection to have chosen the pre-RNA itself rather than any primitive proteins it might be imagined to have produced.

Let me illustrate with antelope. Natural selection can choose an antelope that can outrun predators. Because the slower antelope are more apt to get eaten, the faster ones may leave more and faster offspring. That gives them no ability to make race cars, even though race cars are faster than antelope. This analogy helps us understand that even if natural selection could select for the pre-RNA which was faster at making some reaction happen, this would not give that pre-RNA the ability to make a new thing like an enzyme even though enzymes catalyze (make reactions happen) more rapidly than RNA.

Real RNA cannot have a part in making any protein at all unless it first copies the "blue print" of that protein from DNA. If primitive simple pre-RNA had the information for making all the proteins of the first cell stored within itself, its information storage capacity was far greater than that of real RNA.

Remember that the enzymes which the primitive pre-RNA is to have made are proteins and will not work unless they are folded correctly. At the time I am writing, they are building the super computer Blue Gene because no computer exists which is powerful enough to calculate how proteins fold. This is one more reason why the proposed simple pre-RNA would have required a much greater capacity to store information than real RNA. For pre-RNA to become real RNA later, this capacity would have to have been cut way back. Why would natural selection do that?

Summing up, those who believe in simple pre-RNA have faith that this suggested primitive molecule could:

• Replicate without the help of proteins. (Neither RNA nor DNA can do that.)

• Become capable of making many proteins (none of which would work unless it had been properly folded, addressed to the one spot in which it could connect properly, and carefully regulated as to the amount produced).

• Make DNA.

Real RNA comes in several varieties which work together. Here is what they do:

• Messenger RNA is a copy of a small protein-coding region of DNA that serves as a blueprint for a protein.

• Ribosomal RNA works with specialized proteins as part of a molecular machine that constructs proteins according to the instructions brought by the messenger RNA.

Those who have faith that pre-RNA made the RNA, proteins, and DNA of the first living cell do not base this belief on scientific evidence.

• Transfer RNA places the amino acids in the correct order for the specific protein the molecular machine is making.

Those who have faith that pre-RNA made the RNA, proteins, and DNA of the first living cell do not base this belief on scientific evidence. Most of them have retreated to a belief in pre-RNA because the first choice naturalistic idea (that proteins formed spontaneously) is now widely recognized to be scientifically impossible. It would be even more difficult for RNA to form spontaneously, but that is not yet as well known.

More and more of the best atheistic ideas of how life began are being eliminated. With each new discovery it becomes increasingly evident that life is the work of an intelligent Creator.

DNA

Think of DNA as being shaped like a twisted ladder or a spiral staircase with the letters forming the rungs. This shape is called a double helix. The sides serve to hold the rungs together. (See Figure B.) Instead of being written in ink, or with electrical impulses, DNA has a chemical code. Each of its four "letters" is a different chemical called a base (part of a nucleotide).

RNA is similar. The order of the bases determines the message, much like our messages depend on the order of the letters that make up our words. Like the letters in our words, the bases in DNA and RNA can be put together in any order. Their order is not determined by chemical preferences, but by the message, much like the shape of ink on a page.

Kerkut, a professor who taught evolution to graduate students back in 1960, wrote that several assumptions, none of which can be experimentally verified, form the General Theory of Evolution. I include the first two:

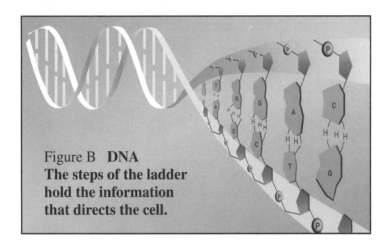

Figure B **DNA**
The steps of the ladder
hold the information
that directs the cell.

"1. Non-living things gave rise to living material, i.e., spontaneous generation occurred.

2. Spontaneous generation occurred only once."[1]

He laid these points out very clearly because he was proposing a contrasting theory. He believed that life on earth had arisen from non-life several times, starting several different lines of plants and animals. (More recently, the punctuated equilibrium movement has given a different explanation for the same lack of transitional fossils between the basic groups of plants and animals). Kerkut's theory lost out when it was discovered that all forms of life on earth are based on DNA. Evolutionists concluded that they all must have evolved from one first cell, though the normal reason for this kind of similarity is intelligent design.

---

[1]G. A. Kerkut, *Implications of Evolution,* 1960, p. 6.

Kerkut was wrong in thinking that life started on several occasions, each of which evolved along separate lines. However, evolution from a common first cell does not go well with much of the evidence either. The Bible gives another possibility, which explains both the similarities and the lack of transitional fossils. It says God created a number of different categories of living things (Genesis 1:11-1:27) rather than one single first cell.

Similarities of design almost always exist when things are made by an intelligent designer. The first automobile had wheels and a motor, as do all automobiles today. Experts use similarities in design to distinguish a house designed by Frank Lloyd Wright from one by Joe Blow, or to recognize paintings by a particular artist. This is a logical explanation for the fact that all living things have DNA. Similarity of design in no way proves that there was no designer, nor that evolution caused the similarities. The fact that motorcycles and automobiles both have wheels is an example. This fact is evidence that both are products of intelligent design, not that one evolved from the other. Whether one believes it came by design or accident, DNA is a recurring theme in living things. A schoolbook states:

> "The genetic code is nearly universal. With few exceptions it is the same in all organisms. For example, the codon GUC codes for the amino acid valine in bacteria, in eagles, in dogs, and in your own cells."[1]

A book written by evolutionists considering the possibility of life on other planets states:

---

[1]George B. Johnson, Peter H. Raven, *Biology, Principles & Explorations*, Holt, Rinehart and Winston, 1996 p. 186.

"...there is a great deal of speculation among scientists about whether DNA is the only molecule on which life can be based or one of many. It is certainly the only one capable of replication and evolution on earth, and all life contains DNA."[1]

Does all life contain DNA because it is so easy to make? Quite the contrary! The same authors state:

"No one has yet discovered how to combine various chemicals in a test tube and arrive at a DNA molecule."[2]

"Some of the steps leading to the synthesis of DNA and RNA can be duplicated in the laboratory; others cannot."[3]

Literature proposing the spontaneous formation of the first life usually does not make clear that DNA and RNA are so difficult to make that some of the steps can't even be done in the laboratory. The problems are often swept under the rug.

Another book comments on the code living things use:

"During the evolution of life on earth, the code was selected as the optimum mechanism for information transfer... and has never been changed or superseded. This provides a striking contrast with modern computer software, which is constantly being updated and superseded."[4]

If it was indeed clay rather than the Creator that selected

---

[1]Ward, Brownlee, *Rare Earth...,* 2000, p. 57.

[2]Ward, Brownlee, *Rare Earth...,* 2000, p. 62, 63.

[3]Ward, Brownlee, *Rare Earth...,* 2000, p. 62, 63.

[4]Shew, Lindsey & Blander, *Lamarck's Signature, How Retrogenes Are Changing Darwin's Natural Selection Paradigm*, 1998, p. 345.

the optimum code for information transfer, and served as a template to pass it on to pre-RNA, I would like to hear some explanation as to how clay could do this.

Why are living cells able to make DNA, RNA, and many proteins? Every cell in your body or in any other living thing has a complete copy of the "instruction book" for that organism which tells how to make the components of each of its cells, and how they must operate. These instructions are found in the cell's DNA. They are written in a language using just four letters instead of 26 like English. Like the letters in a book, the nucleotide bases that serve as the letters in DNA can be arranged in any order. That allows DNA to carry whatever message.

It is easy to understand that almost anything can be written with a four-letter alphabet when we remember that computers work with only two, "off" and "on," sometimes called "0" and "1." Morse code transmits information with just dots and dashes. Anything we can write in English can also be written in code, or on computers. The same information can be transmitted in almost any language, using almost any kind of alphabet.

Since the "writing" of the DNA forms the rungs of the tiny DNA "ladder," we can think of it as a large number of little strips that follow one after another, somewhat like bar code. The letters, among other things, tell the cell the order in which amino acids should be linked together to make each protein the cell needs.

The information "written" in DNA is divided into "chapters" called genes. It was believed that each gene controlled the production of one protein:

"But we found that on average, each human gene seems to make about three different proteins."[1]

The DNA itself is not made of amino acids or protein. Neither is the RNA which copies messages from the DNA and carries them where needed. DNA and RNA are made of nucleic acids; completely different substances than proteins. The relationship is more like that of a blue print to a building. The blue print is not made of the same substance as the building, even though it carries the complete plans for the building's construction.

> **The DNA itself is not made of amino acids or of protein. Neither is the RNA which copies messages from the DNA and carries them where needed. DNA and RNA are made of nucleic acids; completely different substances than proteins. The relationship is more like that of a blue print to a building. The blue print is not made of the same substance as the building, even though it carries the complete plans for the building's construction.**

The big question is, "Where did the cell's 'blue print' come from?" It is written with DNA, but it is more than just nucleic acid, just as a blue print is more than just a rolled up piece of paper with light blue ink on it. Whether a blue print tells you how to build a skyscraper or a shed does not depend on the quality of the paper or the color of the ink, but on the information written on it. One stretch of

---

[1] "The Genome Doctor, an interview with Francis Collins, director of the National Human Genome Institute," *Christianity Today,* 10/1/01, p. 45.

nucleic acids on a strand of DNA will contain the information for making one or more proteins, while the next may not. An entire strand of DNA contains huge amounts of useful information coiled up in a microscopically small space. That undeniable fact brings us to our next, and perhaps most important question:

Where Does Information Come From?

Can chance, matter, or energy compose information or does it always come from an intelligent source? To decide this, we need to agree on what information is. The principle definition of information in my dictionary is, "knowledge communicated or received..." The second is "knowledge gained through study..."[1] Philip Johnson explains how this applies to living things:

> "By information, I mean a message that conveys meaning, such as a book of instructions...
>
> Information is not matter, though it is imprinted on matter...
>
> Instructions in the fertilized egg control embryonic development from the beginning, and direct it to a specific outcome... Similarly, the software in a computer employs natural processes to generate a word processing document, but the software has to be written by an intelligent agent."[2]

The same information can be expressed in a great number of different kinds of codes. It can be stored, or

[1]*Random House Webster's College Dictionary*, 2000, p. 678.
[2]Philip Johnson, *The Wedge of Truth: Splitting the Foundations of Naturalism,* 2000, p. 123, 134.

transmitted as a message. All available evidence indicates that it takes intelligence to invent or create not only meaningful information, but also the alphabets, languages and codes that carry information.

DNA contains meaningful information in a code that can be stored, copied, transmitted, decoded, etc. The DNA of even the simplest cell directs the order in which hundreds of amino acids are strung together to form each of the many proteins a cell needs in order to survive. When one or a few amino acids are out of order, a protein will not work.

How could organic broth know the precise order of each of the amino acids for even one protein, let alone hundreds? The terms "soup" and "broth" refer to a random mixture. Many today pretend that organic broth or clay, or crystals of fool's gold somehow burped out a whole strand of DNA or pre-RNA, and it either came with the information necessary already in it, or with the ability to evolve the encoded information necessary to form not just one, but all of the complex proteins necessary for the first cell. The idea may be a central dogma of the faith of many, but it is certainly not science. It would be comparable to an accident dumping a truck full of old fashioned lead printing type onto the street so that the letters fell out in exactly the order of the letters in the Encyclopedia Britannica.

I write books, and for twelve years directed a publishing house. Could I have simply dipped paper in ink or organic broth and saved the trouble of writing, rewriting, correcting and rewriting? The quantity of information in even a very minimal cell is comparable to that of an encyclopedia. Where did information come from?

When authors propose that DNA evolved from chemicals, they often imply that the material containing the information would have determined the message. If the ultimate source was clay, why would the same clay have passed on the information for making many different proteins? The problem gets worse. The same four nucleotides (letters) code for all the different proteins. If, instead of coming from the clay, the message comes from the material of the DNA itself, the problem is much the same. Why doesn't it make all proteins the same?

The code is obviously determined by the arrangement of these four nucleotides in different orders. To get them into different intelligent sets of instructions requires that they be arranged by an intelligence. Some authors deny that fact to protect their religious or philosophical viewpoint that no intelligent Creator exists. They would be offended if someone told them that the information in their books had been produced by the paper of the book, with no intelligent author involved. At the same time, they claim that the much more complex information in the first cell did indeed come about with no intelligence involved.

Believing that DNA or an imaginary pre-RNA would accidentally come from organic broth or from clay with the correct instructions already on it is like believing the following fanciful explanation of how an encyclopedia could be made in nature: "A storm on the Nile ground up some of the papyrus reed that the ancients used to make paper. The waves deposited some of it on a flat rock where it dried. Now peel it off the rock. Look! It made a sheet of paper! The first encyclopedia must have been formed when a number of these sheets came together." That is like thinking up a story about how RNA could be formed in nature, and claiming to have explained the set of instructions which was written on it. Neither the paper, nor DNA, nor RNA determine the information that will be "written" on them. The author puts the letters in the correct order to transmit the message he chooses.

The material on which the message is written does not determine the message. My old Encyclopedia Britannica was on a CD. Now I consult a copy on the Internet.

Just as the same sheet of paper can be used to draw a comic strip or write a chemical formula, the same stretch of DNA that carries the commands for brown hair can just as easily hold the commands that will make blondes. Or teeth for that matter! DNA's information is real meaningful information. RNA makes copies of portions of it, but it has also been transcribed onto computers in the Human Genome Project, then printed out on paper. The information copied onto the computers carries the same information as the DNA from which it was copied.

Information has also been copied in the opposite direction. High school student Viviana Risca won a $100,000 scholarship from the Intel Science Talent Search for writing the words: "JUNE 6 INVASION: NORMANDY." Why the prize? She wrote them in DNA, using its chemical code![1] The same message that another person can scribble on a napkin at a restaurant or type into a computer, Viviana Risca and others have learned to "write" in DNA.

---

[1]Gungan Singha, *Popular Science,* June 2000, p. 83.

By a process called *genetic engineering*, small bits of information in DNA are now being altered by scientists to make plants that are resistant to bugs or freezing weather. Should we insult these scientists by saying, "That's nothing! Too bad you are not as smart as clay. It invented all the DNA instructions for a whole cell."

Professor Werner Gitt, who works in the field of information science writes:

> "There is no known natural law through which matter can give rise to information, neither is there any physical process or material phenomenon known that can do this."[1]

I believe this statement destroys the whole basis of the idea that no intelligent designer was involved in the formation of the first life.

If a language and letters or some other kind of code had already been provided, perhaps chance action could, if given enough tries, put a few letters together in a meaningful sentence. The first cell, however, had to have a huge carefully planned instruction book that could make and coordinate many complex substances. How did the "letters" of the nucleotides get into the correct order to code for the hundreds of precise proteins which were essential to the life of the first cell? If there had been no intellect involved, would they not have been in one of the millions of possible orders of nonsense gibberish?

Gitt writes that *information is neither matter nor energy. It is another basic kind of thing that needs to be studied.*

---

[1] Werner Gitt, *In the Beginning Was Information,* 1997, p. 79.

He adds:

"• A code is a necessary prerequisite for establishing and storing information.

• Every choice of code must be well thought out beforehand in the conceptual stage.

• Devising a code is a creative mental process.

• Matter can be a carrier of codes but it can not generate any codes."[1]

A few pages later he writes:

"...information cannot be a property of matter; it is always an intellectual construct."[2]

If non-living matter could produce all the information necessary for life, we should see billions of examples of matter creating information. These are not observed.

Someone objected, "How about computers?"

Yes, they are non-living things that contain information, but they only contain information that intelligent people have programmed into them. I remember when people joked that computers with no system or program could be used only as anchors. Computers are lighter weight now, so unprogrammed computers don't even make good anchors any more. In large quantities, unprogrammed RNA or DNA might be useful as dog food, but they could certainly not direct the life of a cell.

A few who don't want to believe in an intelligent Creator have searched for a way to escape the obvious by

---

[1] Werner Gitt, *In the Beginning Was Information,* 1997, p. 67, 65.
[2] Werner Gitt, *In the Beginning Was Information*, 1997, p. 84.

claiming that no real information is associated with DNA. A Nobel Prize winning scientist destroys this argument:

> "In all modern organisms, DNA contains in encrypted form the instructions for the manufacture of proteins. More specifically, encoded within DNA is the exact order in which amino acids, selected at each step from 20 distinct varieties should be strung together to form all of the organism's proteins."[1]

Others claim that the amount of information depends only on the number of letters. They claim that if you add some random letters (nucleotide bases) instead of creating typographical errors, you have increased the information. The more letters, the more information. But not in the book they wrote! Neither does sprinkling ink here and there on a blank page produce meaningful information. Sprinkling ink on a page of text is even worse. The more ink is sprinkled, the more information is covered up. Random ink blots obliterate information, but add none. Those who claim that random marks on a page produce information are often grasping at straws, and purposely confusing static with message in an attempt to save their atheistic faith.

Scientists with the SETI institute are searching for messages from intelligent beings out in space using huge radio telescopes. (The letters "SETI" mean Search for ExtraTerrestrial Intelligence.) They correctly state that *intelligent messages are created only by intelligent beings.* The first step in their search is to separate between static

---

[1]Christian de Duve, "The Beginning of Life on Earth," *American Scientist,* Vol. 83, Sept.-Oct. 1995, p. 430.

and message. So far all they have found is static, but if they find a message from space, they say they will have shown that there are intelligent beings out there. If there are exceptions in which intelligent messages are sent out without any intelligence involved, their whole search is meaningless.

With this in mind, think of DNA. Scientists have found it to be jam packed with intelligent information. This complex information got into the DNA somehow.

Dr. Charles Thaxton helps us understand how important it is to science that presuppositions not be permitted to override the evidence regarding the origin of DNA:

> "If the inference for an intelligent cause for DNA (and for life too, if DNA is truly necessary for life) is in error, than we would likewise be in error to infer the presence of extraterrestrial intelligence upon receipt of intelligible radio messages from deep space. More important, our knowledge of past civilizations provided by archaeologists would be in jeopardy. These supposed "Artifacts" might be, after all, the result of unknown natural causes. Cave paintings, for example... may not be the result of early humans... Indeed, excavated ancient libraries could not be trusted to contain the works of intelligent men and women."[1]

The fact that RNA contains a great deal of information and that DNA contains much more is evidence of an intelligent Creator, not that they were encoded by clay or

---

[1]Charles B. Thaxton, "In Pursuit of Intelligent Causes" *Origins & Design,* Summer 2001, p. 28-29.

organic soup, or by the blind forces of nature. Those who choose to believe the contrary hold to their faith in spite of the evidence, not because of it. The usual reason is that the non existence of a Creator forms a very important part of their world view. Some fear that if they abandon their belief that there is no Creator, their whole belief system may come tumbling down on their heads. If you have this fear, no matter how frightening it may seem, choose truth!

If you are tempted to ask, "Given enough time, couldn't the information of DNA or RNA just happen?" Remember, neither time, nor clay, nor the ocean, produce information. Therefore, more time would not produce more information. It is like asking, "How long would I have to leave my car motor running for it to produce an elephant?" It just does not happen.

Add the creation of information to the long list of things we have studied that cannot happen by chance. Information is produced by intelligence. The fact that DNA contains huge amounts of information is powerful evidence for a very intelligent Creator!

As we will see next, God put His signature on this aspect of His creation by packaging the information written with DNA in the most efficient way possible.

DNA Crams Information into a Tiny Space

Evidence indicates that more information is crammed into less space in DNA than in anything else that exists! The question I am asking you is: If the first cell arose from chemicals without a Creator, how could it have come up with the most efficient container of information imaginable?

The journal *Nature* reported a computer-assisted search

for the best ways of packaging things. It found the tight spiral form of DNA at the top of the list:

> "Such questions of optimal packing are addressed by Maritan et. al. on page 287 of this issue. Some of the optimal shapes they find are the familiar, naturally occurring helical structures of proteins and DNA... Is this an insight or just a coincidence? We suspect it is the former."[1]

What are the chances that a lucky accident provided cells with such an efficient shape for the molecules that contain their information? The fact that the DNA of even the most "primitive" cells is packaged in an optimal shape for efficient packaging is strong evidence that it was designed that way.

An information scientist speaks of a different aspect of DNA's efficiency. He says:

> "DNA molecules contain the highest known packing density of information. This exceedingly brilliant storage method reaches the limit of the physically possible."[2]

Summed up, the coiled shape of the DNA itself packs marvelously well, and the packing density of the information contained inside the DNA "reaches the limit of the physically possible."

Information does not get concentrated in a tiny space by accident. When scientists made the first computers they were huge machines, sometimes taking up whole

---

[1]Andrzej Stasiak and John H. Maddocks, "Best packing in proteins and DNA," *Nature,* Vol. 406, July 20, 2000, p. 251-252.
[2]Werner Gitt, *In the Beginning Was Information,* 1997, p. 195.

buildings, but my laptop stores more information than those early computers. Getting computers small has been a long gradual process, and since their introduction, laptops have traditionally cost twice as much as desktop models with the same capacity. Why? Because the smaller the computer, the harder it is to produce. Does not the fact that DNA started out with the perfect solution for getting the greatest amount of information in the smallest space indicate that it had a very exceptional designer?

We can fit all the information from a whole set of encyclopedias onto one thin CD ROM to place in our computers, and much more on a DVD. That's a lot of information, but we are told that one gram of DNA can hold as much information as a trillion CDs. Whether "a trillion" is a precise number or well rounded, scientists have been inspired by the fantastic storage capacity of DNA.

In addition to its optimal design for information storage, the information in DNA is rapidly available, and is highly resistant to error.[1]

It has been getting easier for us to understand what it means to cram lots of information into a small space. We can fit all the information from a whole set of encyclopedias onto one thin CD ROM to place in our computers, and much more on a DVD. That's a lot of information, but we are told that one gram of DNA can

---

[1]"Tracking the History of the Genetic Code," *Science,* July 17, 1998, p. 281:329-331.

hold as much information as a trillion CDs. Whether "a trillion" is a precise number or well rounded, scientists have been inspired by the fantastic storage capacity of DNA. They are now trying to develop computers that use a molecular approach to overcome the limits of computer chips. If they eventually make a computer as small as a cell with a huge information storage capacity like DNA, and I scoff and claim: "You didn't do that! It just came about by accident," they will rightly consider me a fool. Yet many believe the people who claim that DNA itself was a lucky accident. The Bible says, "The fool hath said in his heart, 'There is no God.'" (Psalm 53:1).

After a number of intelligent scientists had worked for many years developing ever better microfilm they fit the entire Bible on one 32 X 33 mm piece of microfilm. Amazing! However, that space covered with DNA would hold information equivalent to 7.7 million Bibles.[1] If the DNA really did form by accident as biology books often imply, why did it take generations of intelligent scientists thousands of man hours to develop the millions of times less efficient microfilm?

The idea that the random coming together of non-living chemicals produced the information of DNA is preposterous! Atheists, however, don't stop there. They add to that the belief that no intelligence was needed to produce and fill with information the most fantastically efficient tiny container known to man. I wish more Christians had that much faith!

---

[1]Werner Gitt, *In the Beginning Was Information,* 1997, p. 192-194.

The evidence clearly indicates that DNA was designed by a mind far more advanced than ours:

- Information comes only from minds.
- DNA was designed to contain information.
- All cells, even the most "primitive" contain DNA. This indicates that DNA did not gradually evolve, but has existed since living things were first created.
- The information packaging system of DNA is the smallest and most efficient possible. This is true not only of human DNA, but also of that in "primitive" cells. It is so tiny and efficient that scientists cannot yet reverse engineer it and make it in the laboratory. If after 100 more years of study they are able to, will this be evidence that it got into living things with no intelligence involved?

Everyday, people correctly distinguish between things that came about in a random fashion and objects that were designed by humans. They cannot only identify complex objects like jet liners as products of design, but also simple ones like Roman bricks. Many, however, by faith alone, attribute the most complex designs imaginable to mindless processes of nature. Otherwise they might believe in the Creator.

4

Pulling It All Together

How Cells Work

Cells are exceedingly complex, so permit me to offer a simplified explanation which covers only a few of the cell's basic parts. It will provide a framework to which you can add other details as you come across them.

• The DNA is programmed with all the information necessary for the construction and function of the cell. It is the "blueprint" for making the proteins which are responsible for most of the cell structure and its many chemical reactions.

• The ribosomes are little factories that make proteins. There are a number of ribosomes inside each cell. In them, following the instructions in the DNA, proteins and ribosomal RNA fit together in a molecular machine which makes the various proteins needed by the cell.

• Messenger RNA is a copy of a short sequence of DNA. It takes information from the DNA to a ribosome which uses it to make a specific protein. The ribosome only needs a copy of the right "page" of the information in the DNA, not the whole "book."

• Transfer RNA lines up the amino acids in the right order for each protein the ribosome is putting together.

• Enzymes are special proteins that function as catalysts. They speed up chemical reactions. Otherwise these reactions would take place so slowly, if at all, the cell would die while it waited for the first protein to be made.

Here, in a nutshell, is how these parts work together:

The information in the DNA is on the rungs which go from one side of the spiral "ladder" to the other. It is therefore wound up inside the DNA. Some of the enzymes recognize the right spot on the DNA and open up the tightly twisted spiral so the RNA can get at the information it must carry to a ribosome.[1]

> "The central dogma of molecular biology states that information is stored in DNA and flows through RNA to protein."[2]

After the correct part of the DNA has been exposed, a copy is made of just that part. The copy, called messenger RNA, floats over to the ribosome and rubs across it, something like a tape rubs across the head of a tape recorder. As the ribosome is reading these instructions, it is receiving the correct amino acids in the right order and putting them together to make the protein. The address tag

---

[1]C. R. Calladine, Horace R. Drew, *Understanding DNA,* 1997, pp. 65-68, 90.

[2]Karl Drlica, *Understanding DNA and Gene Cloning,* 1997 p. 199.

is added, and as the finished protein comes out of the factory, it proceeds to the spot where it must be to do its job. On the way it is folded to fit the other proteins with which it will work.

Reproduction

The information in the DNA controls a cell's production of its many proteins, RNA, etc. somewhat like a computer running a factory. What happens when a computer is directing the activity of a factory and some really essential part wears out? The factory grinds to a halt! The same thing happens sooner or later to every cell, in spite of its ability to replace many of the parts.

That first cell could not wait a million years to evolve some way to reproduce. The entire system of reproduction had to be fully functional before that first cell died. Otherwise no more life would have existed. The project required a great deal of advanced planning.

Cells, however, unlike factories, are able to reproduce and make new cells before they wear out. Splitting a cell into two cells is done according to a sophisticated plan that requires the interaction of DNA, RNA, and a good number of proteins. What would happen if the DNA (or RNA) of the "first cell" had not already been programmed with the right information to direct its reproduction from the very moment it became a cell? Or what would happen if the information was there, but one of the proteins necessary to perform an essential part of the cell's reproduction did not yet exist?

That first cell could not wait a million years to evolve some way to reproduce. The entire system of reproduction had to be fully functional before that first cell died. Otherwise no more life would have existed. The project required a great deal of advanced planning.

The evidence is stacked against every atheistic fantasy about the spontaneous generation of life. I pray that some of you who read this book will understand; that your eyes will be opened, and you will place your faith in the Creator who not only programmed your DNA, but knows you personally and wants to heal your broken heart and save your soul!

When is a Miracle a Miracle?

If I were to claim that God started life in exactly the same way that is claimed for chance or pre-RNA, atheists would criticize, "This is not science! It would require a miracle at every step. There is no way these things could happen in nature."

The critics would be right! For a first cell to have been formed in the way evolutionists claim would require a whole series of miracles. Some who believe in the spontaneous formation of a first cell have recognized this, and have looked to two billion years to perform the miracle, or to a natural selection that creates, rather than just eliminating the unfit.

Two top first life researchers among the many authors of the influential book *The RNA World*, contrast themselves with the optimistic first life scientists who think impossible things could easily have happened:

"The second group of scientists are much more pessimistic. They believe that the de nuovo appearance of oligonucleotides [Short strings of nucleotides, the building blocks of RNA] on the primitive earth would have been a near miracle. (The authors subscribe to this latter view.)"[1]

Here are a few of the miracles (or near miracles) which would have been required to produce life without a Creator:

• A miracle to provide only left-handed amino acids (and right-handed sugars).

• Another miracle to keep any of them from switching handedness while waiting for the cell to form.

• Another miracle to link them together in the correct order to make each protein.

• Another to address the proteins and send them to the places where each must fit perfectly to connect to those around it.

• It would take a miracle, or a very powerful super computer, to fold each protein correctly so its amino acids could attach properly to those in the proteins around it.

• Another miracle would be required to conceive the huge amounts of information the cell would need, and to program pre-RNA, RNA, and/or DNA with that information.

• What, except another miracle, could invent a cell membrane with the necessary protein channels and pumps

---

[1]G. F. Joyce, L. E. Orgel, *The RNA World*, 2nd ed. 1999, p. 68. (Joyce and Orgel suggest that early gene swapping among pre-RNA strands might somehow have produced the miracle RNA building blocks).

that would provide the environment necessary for the life of a new cell?

• Evolving the mechanism for reproduction in the first cell in the few minutes before it died would require another miracle.

No one who claims these things came about spontaneously in nature is able to make them occur, no matter how sophisticated his laboratory may be. Some Christians have been accused of having a God of the gaps: When they don't understand how something happened, they say that God must have done it. Many who believe in abiogenesis do something much more extreme. They fill the gaps with made up stories about chemical processes that the evidence consistently shows do not happen in nature. Some don't even happen in the lab.

My problem in believing these things is very similar to that of Alice in *Through the Looking Glass*:

"Alice laughed. 'There's no use trying,' she said: 'one can't believe impossible things.'

'I dare say you haven't had much practice,' said the Queen. 'When I was your age, I always did it for half-an-hour a day. Why, sometimes I've believed as many as six impossible things before breakfast…'"

The late Sir Fred Hoyle, the famous astronomer, had the same problem believing the impossible things about the origin of life. After writing: "not one of the many thousands of biopolymers on which life depends could have been arrived at by natural processes here on earth." He speaks of "…a group of persons who believe, quite openly, in mathematical miracles. They advocate the belief that tucked away in nature, outside of normal physics, there is a law which performs miracles (provided the miracles are in the aid of biology.)"[1]

Much good evidence exists that proteins do not form in organic broth, no matter how many amino acids are packed into that broth, nor does pre-RNA form on clay. Neither do DNA, RNA, nor even the nucleotides from which they are made. In essence, a series of small miracles, which we are told are performed by time, natural selection, etc., is being substituted for God's big miracle of the creation of living things. There is no chemical evidence that God did not create life, and He is the only possible source of the information carried in DNA. In addition, in a very reliable ancient document, the Bible, we find God Himself stating that He created: "In the Beginning, God created the heavens and the earth."

But if the principles of chemistry and physics were different, and a first cell did form by naturalistic processes, what would we find? A dead cell! Why do I say that? Every graveyard has trillions of cells full of the right parts. They don't come back to life! Having every necessary part in the same place at the same time is not enough. Something must give the cell life.

Faith in What?

Some have been offended by my above list of the miracles needed to make life. They have responded that they believe science may someday find a way by which a living cell could be created without an intelligent Creator.

---

[1] "The Big Bang in Astronomy," *New Scientist*, Nov. 19, 1981, p. 526, as quoted in Bert Thompson, *The Scientific Case for Creation*, 2002, p. 13.

This is an admission that they hold to their position by faith in spite of the evidence stacked against it. While they have been looking for evidence to confirm their speculation, the growth of scientific knowledge has been turning up more and more evidence for a designer. The cell's information content and its fantastic complexity are among the most important. However, little things are coming to light all the time, like the way proteins must be addressed, folded, and put together to make molecular machines. Most parts work with other parts, and will not work without them. Can you think of any of the cell's complex parts which would be of any use without the other parts?

How much longer will books continue to call it science when they push the evidence aside and present the first life as a simple blob made by chance or clay? If the first simple cell was simple enough for our best scientists to make in the most advanced laboratories, they would be turning out thousands of them.

Designed or Not Designed?

Let's get some things into perspective before we move ahead. Imagine that you are walking down the road and come upon a spot where there had recently been a tremendous wreck. The vehicles have been hauled off, but the road is littered with debris. Among the fragments on the road something captures your attention. Is it a piece of the wreck, or just a chip of rock? You stick it into your pocket and ask a friend who knows cars. He explains: "This is one of the computer chips that control the motor. It checks the sensors, processes the information and gives commands. When the motor is cold, it provides a mixture richer in gasoline than when it is hot. If it detects one thing or another in the exhaust, it uses that information to change the mixture or the timing to make the motor burn more efficiently."

What made the chip? You have two choices:
• It was accidentally put together by the forces of nature.
• It was produced according to an intelligent design.

We recognize things that had to have been conceived by a mind every day, but in all cases in which the designer of a complex object could not be man, we are told that we should not reason like we do for everything else.

You reason: "It receives information from sensors, then it uses the information already contained in the chip to process the information from the sensors and send out commands to the various parts of the motor." You constantly observe intelligent minds creating and using all kinds of information, but you have never heard of chance creating or using information, so you decide the chip is a product of intelligent design.

Every day, we recognize things that must have been conceived by a mind, but in all cases in which the designer of a complex object could not be man, we are told that we should not reason like we do with everything else. We are told that even the most complex things in existence came about by chance or by natural selection with no mind behind them.

We are to "think within the box." The box is called "naturalism." Giving it this label makes it a little less obvious that atheism is becoming the established religion of our schools. The word naturalism has several meanings, but the one that applies in this context is:

"the belief that the natural world, known and experienced scientifically, is all that exists and that there is no supernatural or spiritual creation, control, or significance."[1]

Is this kind of naturalism a religion? Here is the first part of the principle definition of the word "religion" according to the newest dictionary in our house: "a set of beliefs concerning the cause, nature, and purpose of the universe..."[2]

The term "science" once brought to mind knowledge discovered by experimentation, observation and objective investigation. It was to be observable, testable, and repeatable. When one scientist did an experiment, others could repeat his experiment, and obtain the same results.

Should our schools be promoting the naturalistic "beliefs concerning the cause, nature, and purpose of the universe" above all others? How does it differ from promoting the religion of naturalism?

Science Redefined

The term "science" once brought to mind knowledge discovered by experimentation, observation and objective investigation. It was observable, testable, and repeatable.

---

[1]*Webster's New World Dictionary of the American Language,* 1976, p. 947.
[2]*Random House Webster's College Dictionary,* 2000, p. 1116.

When one scientist did an experiment, others could repeat it and obtain the same results. If no one who repeated the experiment came up with the same results, those results had been "falsified," that is, shown not to be true. Under this definition, neither abiogenesis nor evolution are scientific because both are ideas about ancient history, and are not observable, testable, or repeatable. Because of this, and to keep scientists from thinking outside the naturalistic box and coming to non atheistic conclusions, science is being redefined. Many now insist that science must explain all that we observe by solely natural causes.

In Kansas, the state guidelines redefined science as:

> "The human activity of seeking natural explanations for what we observe in the world around us."[1]

Notice, it does not say, "The human activity of seeking the best explanations," or "the most probable explanations" or "the explanations indicated by the evidence." The fact that it says science is the "activity of seeking natural explanations" means that when studying such things as the origin of life, the new definition has already determined the conclusion before the research has even begun! As one philosopher of science puts it:

> "...origin of life research consists in looking for a naturalistic alternative to the idea of the creation of life by a designer."[2]

In reality, the origin of life is outside the bounds of science since it was not observed and cannot be repeated.

---

[1] Peter Keeting, "God and Man in OZ" *George,* Oct. 2000, p. 87.
[2] Iris Fry, *The Emergence of Life on Earth,* 2000, p. 184.

Another problem with the new definition becomes obvious when you try to find a naturalistic alternative to anything you know was designed by a mind: a brick for example. You could say, "Some clay was deposited in a flat spot on the side of a volcano between two straight sided rocks four inches apart. This gave the clay the shape of a brick. The next eruption heated the clay and baked the brick."

Instead of helping us understand how bricks are really made, making up stories about how a brick or an organism might have been made if no intelligence were involved hides the way in which it was really made. Any made up story that indicates a false origin, if assumed to be true, can impede real science.

Police investigating a crime scene find clear fingerprints. Refusing to believe that the one implicated could be guilty, they decide to change the definition of evidence so his fingerprints are excluded. OK! You caught me. It is not cops. I am talking about atheists. Search this book for God's fingerprints. Then notice them in the world around you.

Anyone who accepts a definition for science like, "The human activity of seeking natural explanations for what we observe in the world around us," can only apply it when studying certain specific things. He cannot use this definition when studying anything made by men because his definition only permits him to search among "natural explanations." What was the origin of the chip that controlled the car motor in the illustration at the beginning of this section? Under the new definition, you must reject intelligent design and choose from among natural explanations like: "It broke off a rock," or "It condensed out of hot gasses from a volcano." In one way or another, you must conclude that the subject in question was not made by intelligent minds, but came about by natural causes. The evidence does not matter. You are not allowed to look where the evidence leads when it leads to intelligent design.

If we work under this definition of science, whether we are studying a cell or an automobile, our finding must always be that it had no intelligent Creator. Therefore, the new definition of science: "The human activity of seeking natural explanations for what we observe in the world around us." cannot be used for the huge number of things we observe in the world around us that were made by people. It would lead to answers that are so wrong as to be utterly ridiculous. We can easily test the definition by trying it on objects that we know were made by men. If we do, we will find the new definition to be wrong in every point. Why in the world, then, would we want to put our faith in it in areas where it cannot be put to the test?

To avoid the problem of people putting it to the test, and finding that it does not work, there is an understood exception for cases in which people did the designing. We are expected not to use the new definition in these cases. The test, however, is still valid. A definition of science that will not work in any case where it can be put to the test is obviously faulty. It is interesting that the Bible says:

"So God created man in his own image, in the image

of God created he him; male and female created he them." (Genesis 1:27)

Perhaps the reason man is also able to design things can be found in this statement.

To conclude that living things came about by any kind of spontaneous generation, whether it is rags to rats, protein to life, or the RNA world, requires that all of the evidence which points to intelligent design be thrown out. Throwing out evidence in order to come to a required conclusion is not science.

We can understand the motivation behind the new definition. If one is allowed to follow the evidence for the origin of life wherever it leads, it leads to God. The evidence is so stacked against a mindless source for living things that the only way to arrive at that conclusion is to redefine science!

Some school textbooks have become very persuasive at presenting atheistic speculations in ways that make them sound like science. Belief in any kind of spontaneous generation of the first life, however, is neither belief in science, nor in the evidence, but in a key doctrine of the religions of naturalism, atheism, and agnosticism. Parents who believe in God are being taxed to pay for the books that teach their children a competing religion. If I am wrong, and naturalism has not become the established religion of our schools, in what way does it differ?

Scientists who think outside of the naturalistic box are often disciplined by making it difficult for them to publish the results of their research in scientific journals. Even worse, good scientists and teachers are being fired for simply pointing out some of the real scientific problems with an atheistic or evolutionary approach. An example from our local paper: "A Central Oregon Community College teacher jeopardizes his job by creating doubt about the theory of evolution."[1] This biology teacher was then fired. Such pressure to conform does not encourage honest science, but it may be the only way to get people who recognize design whenever they see it to conform to the idea that the design and information content of cells sprang up without an intelligent designer.

A double standard is being used:

• Things with complex design are accepted as a product of intelligent design if they were made by people, even if the inventor based his product on a design which he found in nature.

If an object with even greater complexity, irreducible complexity, and information content was not designed by a human mind, it is claimed that no mind at all was involved: It must have come about by accident, time, or natural selection. The evidence no longer matters. God has been defined out of existence.

• If an object with even greater complexity, irreducible complexity, and information content was not designed by a human mind, it is claimed that no mind at all was involved: It must have come about by accident, time, or natural selection. The evidence no longer matters. God has been defined out of existence.

---

[1]*The Oregonian,* Feb. 18, 2000, p. D 1, March 28, 2000, p. A 1.

Here is what actually happens when some people examine a cell on a glass microscope slide. I am not making this up. They see the irreducibly complex molecular machines used to manufacture the proteins which form many of the cell's complicated parts. They know that many proteins and at least three kinds of RNA interact precisely with one another to accomplish this process. They know that the cell is equipped to fight off enemies, to transform energy into a usable state, to make and fold proteins so they fit and function perfectly, address them to go to the correct spot in the cell, and turn their production on and off at the right moments. They look at the DNA, which they know contains the huge amounts of complex information that controls all these processes.

Then, undaunted by the fact that only a mind can produce such information and complex design, they insist: "The cell does not show intelligent design."

Now ask these same scientists, "How about the glass slide on which the cell has been laid?"

Without hesitation they answer, "It is a product of intelligent design!"

What good is a microscope to those who refuse to see?

Mount Rushmore

The heads of some of America's most famous presidents were carved out of solid rock on the side of Mount Rushmore. These heads are out in the wind and rain. Someone who knew nothing about them could ask, "Are these heads a natural occurrence? Did weathering and erosion happen to shape the surface of the rock so it resembles the heads of presidents?"

No one asks this question because anything that complex and perfect has obviously been designed. It is the work of a great sculptor. Ask a thousand science teachers. They will all give you the same answer. Yet many of these same teachers stand up in class and teach their students that the very presidents themselves evolved through the blind forces of nature.

These teachers recognize design in a superficial sculpture in which the likeness of a president is not even skin deep, but are blinded to it in the case of the president himself who shows much greater evidence of design as deep as you care to probe.

They can spot design in a flash when it is executed by a person. It doesn't have to be complex like a sculpture, it can be as simple as a brick! They are only blind to evidence of design in things humans did not make; things that might bring them face to face with God.

Looked at superficially, it might seem like someone with a big bucket of camouflage paint dumped it over every design which points to the existence of a Creator. That, of course, is not the reason. Rather:

• Some have a hidden motive. If they don't recognize their Creator, why should they be judged for disobeying His rules?

• Others have a different hidden motive. If your emperor has no clothes, but he doesn't know it, the easy thing to do is to humor him; let him think you agree with him. Otherwise you might not pass the course or get that promotion.

I asked a rather practical engineer, "Why is it that after

our schools have systematically indoctrinated at least three generations in atheistic evolution, polls show that most people today still believe that God created?"

He answered, "Some things are just too self evident!"

Did Life Come from Another Planet?

The probability that something will happen by chance can often be calculated mathematically. Having done the calculations, many scientists and others understand that the evidence is overwhelmingly against life having started on earth without a long string of small miracles, or a Creator capable of making living things all at once. Some have tried to save the idea that the first cell formed spontaneously by moving the action to another planet somewhere else in the universe.

> **Having done the calculations, many scientists and others have understood that the evidence is overwhelmingly against life having started on earth without a long string of small miracles, or a Creator capable of making living things all at once.**

Because I saw how overwhelming the evidence was that life could not have begun on earth without a Creator, I predicted that this idea would become popular in the 1980 edition of my book, *The Creation vs. Evolution Handbook* when the idea of life coming from space was still quite young.

It is more difficult to prove scientifically that life did or did not evolve from non living chemicals on Mars or in some far off galaxy, but I will take a crack at it.

In 1981 Francis Crick, who earlier shared the Nobel Prize for the discovery of the structure of DNA, was struck by the mathematical evidence that life could not possibly have evolved on earth. The probabilities were too strongly against it. While most who believe life came to earth from another planet believe a primitive life form got here on a meteor or a comet, Crick suggested it was sent on purpose on a rocket!

In the same year, the famous astronomer and mathematician Sir Fred Hoyle did a mathematical analysis of the chances of life having evolved:

> "The likelihood of the spontaneous formation of life from inanimate matter is one to a number with 40,000 naughts after it... It is big enough to bury Darwin and the whole theory of evolution."[1]

According to Hoyle, believing that living things were put together by accident was like believing that "...a tornado sweeping through a junk yard might assemble a Boeing 747..."[2]

Some who realize that the first life could not have evolved here have been guiding governments of the world in spending huge amounts of money trying to find life somewhere out in space. Putting the first life farther away works much like the old argument, "In that much time anything could happen." It adds a layer of mystery. We are encouraged to believe: "That far away anything could happen."

---

[1] Hoyle, Sir Fred, and Chandra Wickramasinghe, *Evolution from Space,* 1984, p. 148.
[2] Quoted by Morris and Parker, *What is Creation Science,* 1982, 1996, p. 47-48.

We frequently read, "Life evolves wherever water exists in its liquid form." We are told that with all those galaxies out there, water, and therefore life, must exist on many other planets. It is true that living things require water, just as cars need motor oil. But it does not follow that wherever there is motor oil cars will evolve, nor that wherever there is water, life will evolve.

On the contrary, DNA, RNA, and proteins break down and amino acids switch from all left-handed to a useless half and half mixture more rapidly in the presence of water. In addition:

> "…water greatly interferes with the linking of amino acids and nucleotides into chains, a crucial step in the origin of life. (Chyba 1998:17)"[1]

Long ago, far away, and wet would not make life happen, but would only degrade the materials from which living things are made.[2]

Others have suggested that chemicals needed to make life are probably out there in space:

> "Scientists believe the molecules needed to make a cell's membrane, and thus [needed] for the origin of life, are all over space."[3]

This quote loses track of the fact that the lipids from which complex membranes are made break down all by

---

[1]Iris Fry, *The Emergence of Life on Earth,* 2000, p. 184.

[2]Hendrik E. Poinar, Matthais Hoss, Jeffrey L. Badda, Svante Paabo, "Amino Acid Racemization and the Preservation of Ancient DNA," *Science,* Vol. 272, 10 May, 1996, p. 864.

[3]Louis Allamandola, quoted by Gorman, Jessica, "Cosmic Chemistry Gets Creative." *Science News,* 05/19/2001, Vol. 159, Issue 20, p. 319.

themselves, but even given exactly the right chemicals to make membranes, the lipids do not form. In cells they only form because the DNA contains the program that directs the complex process.[1]

What kind of a planet are they looking for where life might have started? The answer will blow your mind! They are looking for a planet that is just like Earth!

Life also needs a planet that is the right distance from its sun, has the right amount of gravity, the right orbit and speed of rotation, the right atmosphere, temperature, elements etc. Even though earth has all these features, the molecules from which cells are made (lipids, DNA, RNA, proteins) do not form outside of living cells here. The evidence is overwhelmingly against life being generated spontaneously on earth. That is why the theory that life started somewhere else was invented, and why many who do not believe in a Creator are actively searching for a suitable planet somewhere else.

What kind of a planet are they looking for? The answer will blow your mind! A planet that is just like Earth![2]

Information is far more important to the existence of life than water or the other things I have listed. Any living thing must have the plans that tell what it will be, and how it must be made. If the correct information is not contained

---

[1]Iris Fry, *The Emergence of Life on Earth,* 2000, p. 126, 176-177.
[2]Peter D. Ward, Donald Brownlee, Rare Earth, *Why Complex Life is Uncommon in the Universe,* 2000, p. 16, 33.

in the DNA, the evidence indicates that no life can exist,[1] and all known information comes from a mind.[2]

Stanley Miller believes life must have evolved on earth, not in space, because space solves none of evolution's problems, but adds the destructive effects of cosmic rays during the long trip to the earth.[3] Other problems which would be added if life had come to Earth from another planet include the extreme cold of outer space, the lack of anything to breathe during the trip, the time it would take, and the heat and shock of reentry.

Grigg points out two other major obstacles:

"1. The need to achieve escape velocity:

For a rock (or a spacecraft) to break free from the pull of gravity of its mother planet, it must achieve a speed called the escape velocity. For earth this is 11.2 km per second… (25,000 mph). As volcanoes do not eject materials at these speeds, scientists postulate that rocks are blasted from planets and into space through giant asteroid collisions."

"2. The tyranny of distance:

The nearest star to Earth is Proxima Centauri. It is 4.3 light years away… If a planet was orbiting Proxima Centauri and a rock was blasted from it at the speed of earth's escape velocity, the object would take 115,000 years to get here."[4]

---

[1]Ward, *Rare Earth*, 2000, p. 57.
[2]Werner Gitt, *In the Beginning Was Information*, 1997, p. 65, 67, 79, 84, 85.
[3]Stanley L. Miller, *From Primordial Soup to the Prebiotic Beach*, http://www.gene.com/ae/WN/NM/miller.html, 1996.
[4]Russell Grigg, "Did Life Come from Outer Space?" *Creation*, 22 (4), Sept.–Nov., 2000.

All other stars, and any planets they may have, are farther away. If the generally accepted distances are correct, arrival from most stars would take at least millions or billions of years. The temperature during the trip would be near absolute zero, and there would be constant bombardment by cosmic rays. Then, if the alien life form was not burned up on entry into our atmosphere, could it survive the impact with earth?

If life was found on another planet, would that show that life got here from there, or that it got there from here?

At this time, any appeal to life having started somewhere else is another way of saying, "Once upon a time, far far away!" Some who now recognize this fact claim that rather than life coming from outer space, only the raw materials from which life could be made came. Some even cite a slightly higher ratio of left-handed amino acids on a few meteorites. When you read their statements, remember that living things do not just require that more than half of their amino acids be left-handed. They must all be left-handed. In addition, the correct raw materials have been purchased in chemical supply stores, and put together in laboratories. They don't form life. If all left-handed amino acids could be found in space, they would be stuck with the same problems that caused people to look to space in the first place: Amino acids would return to half left and half right-handed. Other materials necessary for life would break down, and for reasons we have already examined, no DNA, RNA, Lipids, or proteins would form.

Before finishing up our discussion on the possibility of life in space, I should again mention the SETI institute.

The scientists of the institute are using huge radio telescopes to search for intelligent beings in space. They reason that if intelligent life exists outside our earth it would be reasonable to expect it to try to communicate with us. The SETI scientists know that intelligent information can be produced only by intelligent beings. They believe that an intelligent message from outer space would be conclusive evidence for the existence of an intelligent being out there somewhere.

> **The SETI scientists know that intelligent information can be produced only by intelligent beings. They believe that an intelligent message from outer space would be conclusive evidence for the existence of an intelligent being out there somewhere.**

Like the SETI scientists, Dr. Gitt has studied the evidence for the origin of information, and he also is convinced that all known information comes from a mind. He said this in discussing the information contained in DNA.

Archeology is another area of science largely based on the fact that information only comes from minds. Archeologists count on it when they identify the inscriptions on stacks of clay tiles they have dug up in a library produced by intelligent people. The fact that the DNA of every living cell has been programmed with huge amounts of intelligent information written in the most efficient manner ever discovered is evidence of the existence of an intelligence greater than that of the people who inhabit our planet. Some people, to avoid admitting this powerful evidence for an intelligent Creator, insist that the information in DNA comes from matter, or some other source rather than a mind. If true, their argument would also destroy the SETI institute and the science of archeology. It obviously is not true.

The Meaning of Life

Chemistry Professor Andrew Ellington states his position as an evolutionist with great literary force:

"We are borne of slime layers on rocks…"[1]

According to Ellington, you evolved from slime by an accident of nature. If he is right, all that makes life noble and gives it purpose is gone. We might as well have remained slime! Is he right? Slime + time =?

Life comes from life. That is a scientific principle. Getting something from nothing for no reason is not scientific. It is contrary to several scientific principles and laws.

No matter how convincing the evolution of a first living cell can be made to appear, it is still the fisherman's story of the big one that got away. Not even in the best equipped laboratory has anyone ever created a cell. No matter how many books state or imply the opposite, not even the cell's principle components are produced in nature except when made by already living cells. Life comes from life. That is a scientific principle. Getting something from nothing for

---

[1]The *Probability of Abiogenesis,* Asst. Prof. of Chemistry Andrew Ellington 1995, http://earth.ics.uci.edu/faqs/faq-abiogenesis.html.

no reason is not scientific. It is contrary to several scientific principles and laws. Our Creator is alive and our life comes from Him.

Taking God out of the schools and replacing Him with slime, clay, and organic broth has left a void. Attempts are being made to fill that void with expensive metal detectors and police patrols, but when kids are convinced they have no souls and are only moving from slime on a rock to dust in a grave, they have no hope. Darwinism is the grinch that stole hope. Guns in school are just a symptom. Whether kids turn them on themselves, or shoot others to go out in a blaze of glory, they are expressing a sort of backhanded compliment. The lesson they have been taught at school has gotten through. Many believe there is no God, no heaven or hell, no salvation, no purpose in life, and no hope.

Another scientist, looking at life from his position as an evolutionist, gives the hopelessness a different slant:

> "It is very hard to admit that there is only one single reason for each of us to come into this world: to transmit our DNA to the next generation. There is absolutely no other purpose for us to be born."[1]

If he is right, any moral rules that limit our sexual activity hinder us in accomplishing the "one single reason for each of us to come into this world."

The Ten Commandments have been thrown out of the schools. Not just the commandments against lying and murder, but also the one against adultery. Some people who don't believe that the only reason we were born was

---

[1]Maxim D. Frank-Kamenetskii, *Unraveling DNA,* 1997, p. 130.

to transmit our DNA, get on the band wagon with those who want to have God and His commandments thrown out of the schools so they can take advantage of the resulting loose moral standards.

Many evolutionists are honest people with high moral standards, but can you think of a clear basis for morality in the evolutionary viewpoint? Provine, a well known evolutionist wrote:

> "Evolution provides no foundation for ethics and no deep meaning in life."[1]

If selection of the fittest really is making us into better and better animals because the strong replace the weak, why should we not be the strong, and murder, tell lies and commit sexual immorality before we are eliminated in the fight to survive because someone else has done that to us?

The evidence, however, shows that God does exist! He explains that He is a righteous Judge, and says; "It is appointed unto men once to die, but after this the judgment" (Hebrews 9:27). When Jesus was asked, what is the most important commandment, He answered:

> "Thou shalt love the Lord thy God with all thy heart, and with all thy soul, and with all thy mind. This is the first and great commandment. And the second is like unto it, Thou shalt love thy neighbor as thyself." (Matthew 22:37-39)

The only bad thing is that because of God's commandments

---

[1]Provine, W.B. "Progress in Evolution and Meaning in Life," In Nitecki (editor), 1985, p. 72, quoted by ReMine, Walter J. *The Biotic Message,* 1993, p. 157.

we know we have not lived as He asks, and we risk His judgment. The next chapter will explain His provision for us in this dilemma. It is much better than distorting science to pretend He does not exist. God, who asks us to love each other, has provided for our sin and empowers us to live as we should. You are not slime. There is hope! God loves you and has a fine purpose for your life. He not only created man, He knows you personally and wants to save your soul and heal your broken heart. Life is great when you let the Creator care for you and lead you day by day.

5

The Message

We have seen one evidence after another that life could not have been a chance occurrence but must have been created by an intelligent being. Remember the SETI scientists and their insistence that only intelligent beings create the information in meaningful messages? I used their statement before because it helps us understand the source of the information in DNA.

Now I want to point out their belief that if intelligent life exists somewhere other than on earth, it might try to communicate with us. These scientists have been pointing the world's largest radio telescopes out into space, looking for a radio message. The bad news is they have not found one.

The good news is that another message has already been delivered. To make sure we could understand, God became a person, Jesus Christ, and lived for a time right here on earth. He showed who He was by doing miracles no one else could do.

True, throughout history many have not believed. In fact, many have hated Him. When He was a small child, an evil king tried to kill Him by having all the children of His age in His town killed. When He grew up and brought forth His message, the religious leaders rejected Him and when the time came for the Lord to lay down His life for our sins they had Him killed. However, after three days He rose from the dead and sent His followers out to deliver His message, which still lifts people from degraded lives of sin to lives of peace and sterling character.

The Ten Commandments, that have been thrown out of many public places, show us we are sinners who have not kept God's laws. Christ explained how we can be saved from having to suffer God's judgment on sin. His death paid the penalty for our sin.

The story of God becoming a man to bring us this message is recorded in the Bible, which is a message to us from our Creator. He gave it to us in written form which we can examine for ourselves. Can I back up this statement with evidence? Yes, here is some:

Though originally written in three languages by more than 40 writers over a period of more than 1500 years, the 66 books of the Bible agree with each other just as they would if they were all inspired by one mind as the Bible claims. This is not true of other books, ancient or modern:

• It would be hard to find a scientific specialization that agrees now with what was taught even 50 years ago.

• The history of philosophy is the story of each successive philosopher's thoughts which he defended by showing how those before him had been wrong.

• In writing this book I had to use very recent quotes from scientists because science changes so rapidly.

• The next time you are seriously sick, how would you like to be treated by the medicine of just 100 years ago?

Science and philosophy change rapidly, yet the 66 books of the Bible agree among themselves so well that we often think of the Bible as one book. Try to find other books which were written over a period of 1500 years that agree with one another. Impossible, isn't it? Can you find them for even 200 years? 100?

What Book is Number Two?

I did an informal poll asking many people: "What is the second most important book in the world?" Almost everyone knows the Bible is the most important book, but the book that comes in second is so far behind, nobody can agree what book it would even be. Whether you love or hate the Bible, it stands out from other books.

Many more ancient copies of the Bible were made and preserved than of any other really old book. Why? In the past, as today, many believed it was the Creator's message to man.

Another way in which the Bible stands out is that it is still in print. Even though publishing today is cheaper and easier than ever, most manuscripts submitted to publishers are still rejected. Of those that do get published, only around one in 50 goes into a second edition. Even the fortunate books that go into many editions eventually lose the public interest, and are no longer published.

Except the Bible!

After the Bible had been copied by hand for well over a thousand years, Gutenberg invented the printing press that printed copies of the Bible more rapidly. Since then, its distribution has grow constantly. Almost 2000 years have passed since its writing was completed, and every year more copies of the Bible are sold than of any books which might be considered next in importance.

The Old Testament was one of the first major books to be translated into a second language: into Greek around the time of Christ. The Bible has since been translated into many more languages than any other book. At the end of the year 2000, of the 6,809 languages in the world, the entire Bible had been translated into 383 languages. Another 987 have only the New Testament, and another 891 languages have at least one complete book of the Bible.[1]

When you finish reading most books, they sit on the shelf collecting dust, yet millions of people read the Bible again and again. Some of us read portions of it every day. Why? Because of the nature of God's communication with us. Little children who read the Bible understand a good deal, but adults find it so profound there is always more to learn and put into practice.

The Bible has been quoted more often and has inspired more commentaries, films and literature than any other book. Why is all this true of the Bible, but no other book? Would it not be wise to at least consider the reason the Bible itself offers, that it is the word of God?

---

[1]Information from the Portland office of the Wycliffe Bible Translators.

After reading all this, many will feel a rage against the Bible building up, and some of you will understand from personal experience that the Bible is not only the most loved book in the world, but also the most hated. Why? Perhaps for some because the Bible's first words are: "In the beginning, God created the heavens and the earth." While the statement is logical, some people hate the idea of a Creator who has a right to ask them to love Him and live for Him.

Whatever the reasons, there have always been those who oppose the idea that the Bible is a message from God to man. Many strongly contest the words of Christ: "Heaven and earth shall pass away: but my words shall not pass away" (Mark 13:31). Even these folks must admit that Christ's words have held up remarkably well for the first 2000 years.

John Wycliffe was the first to translate the Bible into English. After his death, officials who did not want others to be able to read the Bible were so irritated that they dug up his body and burned it. William Tyndale, who produced the second English translation, was imprisoned for a year and a half, then tied to a stake, strangled, and his body was burned.[1]

Throughout history, many times more people have been tortured and killed for reading the Bible than for reading any other book. In more recent times, communist nations have burned and torn up millions of Bibles, often imprisoning people just for having one.

---

[1]*Fox's Book of Martyrs*, 1926, p. 184.

Sometimes those who attack the Bible feel they have finished it off for all time. Voltaire, a famous skeptic of an earlier day, was one of these. He predicted that within one hundred years after his attacks, the Bible would disappear from circulation. Instead, just fifty years after his death, his own house became a warehouse for Bibles.

Viggo Olsen, a brilliant doctor, and his wife were more recent skeptics. They read and followed the works of the famous skeptics of their day. They were challenged by Christians to search for the truth, and agreed because of a hidden motive:

> "But our agnostic bias made us begin the 'search' in a diabolically clever way. We would prove the Bible is not the word of God, that Christianity is not the true religion of God, and that Christ was but a man, not the Son of God!"[1]

The critics they had been following cited as their proofs of errors in the Bible the absence of archeological finds confirming the existence of:

• The Hittites and Edomites. The critics called them "legendary people" while the Bible identified them as real ancient tribes.

• "...the Roman census which brought Joseph and Mary to the town of Bethlehem, where Jesus was born..."

Critics also claimed that the Bible made these and other mistakes because its books were written in periods of history hundreds of years later than those claimed by the

---

[1]Viggo Olsen, *Daktar/diplomat in Bangladesh,* 1973, p. 33.

books themselves. Most importantly of all, critics claimed that writing was not yet known in Moses' time so Moses could not have written the five books of Moses. What did the Olsen's investigation lead them to conclude?

"Contrary to our previous understanding, we found the Bible to be historically accurate."[1]

In addition to reading the Bible itself, Olsen checked out recent archeological finds and found that the points he and other skeptics were using as proofs against the Bible were out of date. Archeological research had already shown the Bible to be true in each of these points.[2]

Writing not only existed in Moses' time, but whole libraries had been unearthed from before his time. Archeology has also shown that the authors of the Bible had a knowledge of the times in which they claimed to write that would be virtually impossible for anyone of a later time to acquire.

It is true that some things the Bible speaks of have not yet been confirmed by archeological digging, but most of the accusations against the Bible that I hear being passed around today are old accusations that archeologists have long ago shown to be in error.

The Olsens approached the Bible thinking that if salvation existed, it would be merited by those who had not sinned. As they read, however, they found that Christ came to save sinners... He died to save them from their sins, and proved it by rising from the dead.

---

[1] Viggo Olsen, *Daktar/diplomat in Bangladesh,* 1973, p. 45; 33-49.
[2] Viggo Olsen, *Daktar/diplomat in Bangladesh,* 1973, p. 45.

After careful study, the Olsens were convinced and trusted Christ to forgive their sins. They accepted the salvation that He offered. Their lives were transformed, and dedicated to serving God.[1]

The former skeptic became a medical missionary in Bangladesh, one of the most needy places on earth. Why? Because in addition to having made the Bible difficult to prove wrong, God also uses it to change lives. Read it and you may find out what this means.

Josh McDowell was also challenged by Christians to examine the claims of Christ. He thought Christians were idiots, and believed if he could write a book laying to rest once and for all the myths Christians believed, his book would become a best seller. He studied the evidence from history, archeology and ancient literature and wrote, not one, but many books. He laid out good solid evidence. His books, however, show that Josh McDowell had been wrong, and the Bible right![2] Christ really did die on the cross for our sins, and He did rise from the dead. Many witnesses really did see Him. When Josh realized these things, he too trusted Christ, and dedicated his life to serving his Lord.

In the past, more archeologists have gone out searching for evidence against the Bible than against any other book. Josh learned that many of these same archeologists have

---

[1]Viggo Olsen, *Daktar/diplomat in Bangladesh,* 1973, p. 50-54.
[2]I particularly recommend *More than a Carpenter, The Resurrection Factor, Answers to Tough Questions, Evidence that Demands a Verdict,* and *A Ready Defense.*

ended up praising its accuracy. Dr. Nelson Glueck, an outstanding Palestinian archaeologist, said:

"It may be stated categorically that no archaeological discovery has ever controverted a Biblical reference. Scores of archeological findings have been made which confirm in clear outline or in exact detail historical statements in the Bible."[1]

Famous archaeologist W.F. Albright, recipient of over twenty honorary degrees, wrote:

"Archaeological and inscriptional data have established the historicity of innumerable passages and statements in the Old Testament..."[2]

Step up to the challenge like Olsen and McDowell did. Why should you trust the critics and reject the Bible without comparing their relative track records?

The Bible's critics often charge that its central message, the story of Jesus Christ, is a myth or it would have been mentioned in other ancient literature besides the Bible. Actually Jesus Christ *is* mentioned in other ancient literature. Check it yourself! The many volumes referred to as "The Church Fathers" give Christ a great deal of friendly testimony, but He is also mentioned in several ancient books written by His enemies. I quote a few:

---

[1] Olsen, p.46, quoted from Henry M. Morris, *The Bible and Modern Science,* 1968, p. 95.
[2] W. F. Albright, *The American Scholar,* Publication of Phi Beta Kappa, Vol. 7, No. 2, Spring 1938. See also Albright, *The Archeology of Palestine and the Bible,* 1974, p. 128-129; *The Archeology of Palestine,* 1954, p. 219-237.

The Romans:

• Tacitus, AD 110, in his account of the persecution of Christians, Tacitus explains: "The name is derived from Christ, whom the procurator Pontius Pilate had executed in the reign of Tiberius."[1]

• Pliny the Younger, governor of Asia Minor, AD 111-112, asks in a letter to the emperor Trajan how he should treat the Christians. McDowell explained: "...he had been killing both men and women, boys and girls. There were so many being put to death that he wondered if he should continue killing anyone who was discovered to be a Christian, or if he should kill only certain ones."[2]

• Suetonius, A. D. 112.[3]

The Jews:

• The Talmud contains a few statements from the first and second centuries A. D. which refer to Christ.

• The Jewish historian Josephus, Antiquities of the Jews, A. D. 93, 18:3:3.

The *Encyclopedia Britannica* sums up its list of ancient statements about Jesus from non Christian sources:

> "These independent accounts prove that in ancient times even the opponents of Christianity never

---

[1]Annals of the Roman historian Tacitus (XV, 44) from *Encyclopedia Britannica,* "Jesus Christ, The gospel tradition, Non-Christian sources."
[2]Pliny the Younger, Epistle 10, 96 ff. From *The Best of Josh McDowell, A Ready Defense,* compiled by Bill Wilson, 1990, p. 200, see also *Encyclopedia Britannica,* Jesus Christ, The Gospel Tradition, Non-Christian sources.
[3]Vita Claudii, 25:4, see also Lives of the Caesars, 25.2.

doubted the historicity of Jesus, which was disputed for the first time and on inadequate grounds at the end of the 18th, during the 19th, and at the beginning of the 20th centuries."[1]

John Clifford wrote a well known poem summarizing the result of the attacks on the Word of God by the critics:

"Last eve I passed beside a blacksmith's door,
And heard the anvil ring the vesper chime.
Then looking in, I saw upon the floor,
Old hammers, worn with beating years of time.

'How many anvils have you had,' said I,
'To wear and batter all these hammers so?'
'Just one,' said he, and then with twinkling eye;
'The anvil wears the hammers out, you know.'

'And so,' thought I, 'the Anvil of God's Word,
For ages skeptic blows have beat upon;
Yet, though the noise of falling blows was heard,
The Anvil is unharmed, the hammers gone.'"

The Bible has withstood the continual hammering of the critics. Throughout history many like Voltaire, Olsen, and McDowell have tried to destroy the Word of God. What have their hammers accomplished? More copies of the Bible are selling in more languages than before the critics picked up their hammers. Why does it fare so much better than your book or mine? Is it just a lucky accident, or is

---

[1]*Encyclopedia Britannica,* Jesus Christ, The Gospel Tradition, Non-Christian Sources.

there really something different about the Bible? Read it regularly. "Is not my word like as a fire? saith the LORD; and like a hammer that breaketh the rock in pieces?" (Jeremiah 23:29)

Would You Like to Be Rich?

Let me give you a tip on a sure way to get rich. All you need is the ability to see just one day into the future. Try it! You can become incalculably rich just by buying and selling stock. If you know that Microsoft or General Electric will take a big jump up in price tomorrow, buy that stock today. Do it consistently, and before long, the rulers of the world will be lined up at your door begging for loans.

Can't get rich on the stock market because you can't see a day into the future? Don't despair! There is a way to get rich if you can only see ahead a minute or two. Play the horses!

If minutes are too long, you only need to look into the future a few seconds to get rich in the gambling casinos.

It's a nice dream, but no one can see into the future. We know that because anyone who could, would already own almost everything.

God claims He spoke in the Bible about certain things before they happened so that when they happened we would know it was He who had caused them:

> "Because I knew that thou art obstinate... I have even from the beginning declared it to thee; before it came to pass I showed it thee: lest thou shouldest say, Mine idol hath done them..." (Isaiah 48:5)

In saying this, God is challenging us to put Him to the test in the area of prophecy. When we do, we find that His Word has foretold many things men could never have known. This builds up our faith in what He says about other things as well. Some who refuse to believe that God can see the future claim that the very accurate prophesies of the Bible were actually faked prophesy written by others much later, after the facts had already occurred. Let's examine an Old Testament prophesy about Christ that, for a number of reasons, could not have been faked later.

Isaiah 53

This prophesy of Jesus Christ was written around 700 B.C. How do we know it was not faked after the time of Christ? In 1947 the first of the famous Dead Sea Scrolls was found in caves in the desert near the Dead Sea. Books of the Bible were among the older of the Dead Sea Scrolls.[1] Though many were fragmentary, among them was a copy of the entire Book of Isaiah made around 100 B.C.[2] A large portion of another copy of Isaiah and a number of smaller fragments were also among the scrolls. We know Isaiah's prophesy of Christ was not faked after the time of Christ because the copy of the whole book, made 100 years before Christ's birth, still exists today. It remained sealed in a jar in a desert cave until 1947. It has been photographed so if you know Hebrew you can compare it

---

[1]Encyclopedia Britannica (on line), Dead Sea Scrolls.
[2]Unger's Bible Dictionary, 1957, p. 253; Millar Burrows, Burrows on the Dead Sea Scrolls, 1978, p. 118; Baker Encyclopedia of the Bible, Vol. 2, 1988, p. 598.

to the copy in your own Bible. The Isaiah Dead Sea scrolls say the same thing that we are going to study from the Old Testament of our English Bible, so no one can successfully argue that the prophesy we are about to examine was faked after Jesus had already done the things prophesied. Long before Christ came to earth, God really did tell us many of the things He was going do, so when they had happened, we would believe.

To be brief, we will start with Isaiah 53:5, but I encourage you to read all of chapter 53 in your own Bible:

> "But he was wounded for our transgressions, he was bruised for our iniquities: the chastisement of our peace was upon him; and with his stripes we are healed." (Isaiah 53:5)

The passage I have chosen is central to God's message to man. It speaks of Christ suffering for us. The following verses include one detail after another of Christ's death and resurrection. Each one makes the prophesy fit Jesus more specifically. This passage can only describe Jesus Christ. No one else in history meets the criteria.

Notice how the next verse gives us further insight into why God the Father laid our punishment on Christ:

> "All we like sheep have gone astray; we have turned every one to his own way; and the LORD hath laid on him the iniquity of us all." (Isaiah 53:6)

Because we had wandered off instead of following God, Christ carried our sin in His sacrifice for us. You may remember that at His trial Christ did not defend Himself:

> "He was oppressed, and he was afflicted, yet he opened not his mouth: he is brought as a lamb to

the slaughter, and as a sheep before her shearers is
dumb, so he openeth not his mouth." (Isaiah 53:7)

We have already seen that Christ carried our sins, but up
to this point the passage had not spelled out the fact that
He would actually die for them. God was getting to that:

"...for he was cut off out of the land of the living:
for the transgression of my people was he stricken"
(Isaiah 53:8).

Isaiah 53 is a preview of the Gospel which would be
explained seven hundred years later in the New Testament.
Christ died for our transgressions. The verses we saw
before put it: "for our iniquities," because we have "gone
astray." God sees our sins as so serious that only the death
of His Son could pay for them.

The next verse gives our faith another big jump by
adding details about his burial that make the prophesy even
more specific, and less likely to have just been a lucky
coincidence:

"And he made his grave with the wicked, and with
the rich in his death..." (Isaiah 53:9)

How was this verse fulfilled? The most powerful nation
on earth at the time intended to have Jesus buried with the
wicked men who were crucified with Him. However, at the
last moment, a rich man went to the Roman ruler and
received permission to bury Christ's body in the new tomb
he had dug for himself (Matthew 27:57-60).

Next, Christ's resurrection, was foretold:

"...when thou shalt make his soul an offering for
sin, he shall see his seed, he shall prolong his
days..." (Isaiah 53:10)

The precision of Bible prophesy is a real problem to anyone who refuses to believe, so some have claimed that Isaiah 53 was not talking about Christ. This verse, however, destroys their position. Who else died and then prolonged his days? Christ rose again from the dead! Remember, we know that this prophesy was written long before Christ came because handmade copies had already been hidden in caves near the Dead Sea many years before He died and rose again.

This verse also answers those who claim: "Jesus was not the Savior. He just knew the prophesies regarding the Messiah and arranged His life to accomplish things that had been foretold so people would think He was the Messiah." Few impostors would purposely get themselves killed by crucifixion, and none could rise from the dead.

Another prophesy names the town where Christ would be born. When the wise men came not long after His birth asking where Jesus was born, the wicked King Herod was able to tell them. To do this he simply inquired of those who knew the Scriptures: "And they said unto him, In Bethlehem of Judaea: for thus it is written by the prophet." (Matthew 2:1-8, Micah 5:2). An impostor could not arrange the town where he would be born.

Christ's family tree was also spelled out in prophesy. He was from the family of Abraham (Genesis 22:18, Galatians 3:16), more specifically from the tribe of Judah, (Genesis 49:10), and from the house of David (Isaiah 11:1, Jeremiah 23:5, 33:15).

Another prophesy says that at His death evil men would pierce his hands and feet and divide up His clothes (Psalm

22:16-18). No impostor could arrange his life to fulfill such prophesies.

Someone might say, "OK, it was prophesied that Christ would die and rise from the dead, but I don't believe he really came back to life."

Christ's disciples felt that way too! Several times before His death, Christ had told his disciples that he would be crucified and then rise from the dead (Matthew 20:19, John 2:18-22). However, they refused to believe His resurrection predictions, so when He died, their hope died with Him. They had really believed that Jesus Christ was the long expected Messiah, so when He died, they were demoralized. Even when some women came back and reported that He had risen from the dead, the disciples refused to believe their testimony. Only later, when they saw Him themselves, did they believe.

After that, Thomas, who was not there when Christ appeared, told his fellow disciples that he would not believe unless he could touch Jesus' wounds. Jesus came to the disciples again when Thomas was present. He told Thomas to reach out and feel His wounds. Thomas believed. Jesus said,

> "Thomas, because thou hast seen me, thou hast
> believed: blessed are they that have not seen, and
> yet have believed. (John 20:21)

Christ was later seen alive by more than five hundred witnesses. After the disciples saw and touched Him, and received the Holy Spirit as Jesus had promised, these men who had been demoralized, depressed, disillusioned and disheartened, were transformed and went everywhere, boldly preaching that Jesus had been raised from the dead. (Mark 16:9-11, Luke 24: 19-21, Acts 4:1-3, 7:57-8:3) The opposition to their message was so fierce that most of them were eventually killed because they stuck to their testimony that Christ had come back to life.

If the resurrection was not true and Christ was still dead, what transformed the disciples? They would have stayed discouraged. It would have been most strange for them to go out and be killed for their testimony that He had come back from the dead. Because they saw, they believed, and the Holy Spirit empowered them.

Acts 8:30-38 tells of a government official who, returning to Ethiopia after a visit to Jerusalem, was seated in his chariot reading the same prophesy of Christ in Isaiah 53 which we just read. God sent Philip to explain this passage to him. The official trusted Christ and was baptized. After reading the same prophesy, you too now know that the Bible is not just another of men's books, but is the word of God. Christ paid in full the penalty for your sins. I pray that you might receive Him just like that official. The next verse explains how:

> "by his knowledge shall my righteous servant justify many; for he shall bear their iniquities." (Isaiah 53:11)

By knowing Him you can be justified and have peace with God:

> "Therefore being justified by faith, we have peace with God through our Lord Jesus Christ" (Romans 5:1)

Christ died bearing your sins and mine. Why not trust him like that official?

"For all have sinned, and come short of the glory of God; being justified freely by his grace through the redemption that is in Christ Jesus." (Romans 3:23-24)

You may find it hard to believe that God would really forgive a person who has done the things you have done. Remember, however, two criminals were executed along with Jesus. Even at the very end, one of them insulted Christ and refused to believe. You could follow this man's example, refuse Christ, and be condemned to eternal suffering in hell, but why would you want to do that? Why not follow the example of the other criminal who prayed:

"Lord, remember me when thou comest into thy kingdom."

"And Jesus said unto him, 'Verily I say unto thee, today shalt thou be with me in paradise.'" (Luke 23:42-43)

Wouldn't you like to pray this same prayer and be with Jesus when you die? The mighty God who created the universe and life itself invites you to become His child; to be clothed in the goodness of Christ, and not in your own sin when you stand before Him at the Judgment. How can you be clothed in Christ's purity and not your own sin?

One of my sons is an industrial electrician. Sometimes he works in a factory that makes wafers that are cut up to make computer chips. Everything must be kept spotless because the circuits in the chips are so tiny that even a small speck of dust could ruin a chip. No one can enter the clean rooms without a special suit that does not produce dust. My son does not even own such a suit. How can he work there? No problem! The factory provides it. When they tell him he must wear this special suit or he can't go in, all he has to do is believe them, accept it, and put it on.

God's heaven is clean too. You can't go there clothed in your sin, but God loves you and offers you Christ's righteousness and goodness. That is what it takes to get into heaven. Don't wait. Accept. When you realize Christ died for your sin and rose again, the most logical thing you can do is to repent and trust Him to save you. This very moment, tell God that you have sinned against Him and His law, and trust Christ to take away your sin and clothe you in His righteousness.

While you can't see clearly into the future, and may never have the riches of this world, in Christ you will find the riches that really count:

"For ye know the grace of our Lord Jesus Christ, that, though he was rich, yet for your sakes he became poor, that ye through his poverty might be rich. (2 Corinthians 8:9)[1]

Accept the riches that are being offered to you right now by the Creator of heaven and earth; your Creator, your Savior!

---

[1]For further information, see the books of John, Romans, and Galatians in the Bible.

Index